Leaders of the Colonial Era

John Smith

Leaders of the Colonial Era

Lord Baltimore

Benjamin Banneker

William Bradford

Benjamin Franklin

Anne Hutchinson

Cotton Mather

William Penn

John Smith

Miles Standish

Peter Stuyvesant

John Smith

Tim McNeese

An imprint of Infobase Publishing

Chelsea House
An imprint of Infobase Publishing
132 West 31st Street
New York, NY 10001

Library of Congress Cataloging-in-Publication Data
McNeese, Tim.
  John Smith / Tim McNeese.
    p. cm. — (Leaders of the colonial era)
  Includes bibliographical references and index.
  ISBN 978-1-60413-742-2 (hardcover)
  1. Smith, John, 1580–1631—Juvenile literature. 2. Colonists—Virginia—Jamestown—Biography—Juvenile literature. 3. Explorers—America—Biography—Juvenile literature. 4. Explorers—Great Britain—Biography—Juvenile literature. 5. Jamestown (Va.)—History—17th century—Juvenile literature. 6. Jamestown (Va.)—Biography—Juvenile literature. 7. Virginia—History—Colonial period, ca. 1600–1775—Juvenile literature. I. Title. II. Series.
  F229.S7M38 2010
  973.2'1092—dc22
  [B]   2010010334

You can find Chelsea House on the World Wide Web at
http://www.chelseahouse.com

Text design by Kerry Casey
Cover design by Keith Trego
Composition by EJB Publishing Services
Cover printed by Bang Printing, Brainerd, Minn.
Book printed and bound by Bang Printing, Brainerd, Minn.
Date printed: November 2010
Printed in the United States of America

10 9 8 7 6 5 4 3 2 1

This book is printed on acid-free paper.

All links and Web addresses were checked and verified to be correct at the time of publication. Because of the dynamic nature of the Web, some addresses and links may have changed since publication and may no longer be valid.

Contents

1

A Man of Adventure

John Smith was a commoner by birth, one whose destiny would normally have remained tied to the English land as a farmer. He was born on January 9, 1580, an exciting time for exploration. Four years earlier, English explorer and sea captain Martin Frobisher had sailed to North America in search of gold and the Northwest Passage but had failed to find either. When Smith was only three years old, Frobisher's sponsor, Sir Humphrey Gilbert, had himself sailed to the New World to establish an English colony, along with seven ships and 400 men, only to be lost at sea. Smith was only five years old when the first English colony in America, Roanoke, was established on an island off modern-day North Carolina, only to collapse, be reestablished two years later, then completely disappear by the time young Smith turned 10.

During the years of England's attempts to establish a permanent colony in North America, with all efforts ending in failure, John Smith was just a boy.

His father was a relatively prosperous landowner who owned pasture land in Great Carlton, as well as property in the nearby market town of Louth. Already feeling the farm life was not for him, he was inclined "even then . . . upon brave adventures." His first "brave adventure" was to apprentice himself to a willing merchant in the town of King's Lynn in Norfolk. Under their agreement, Smith was to serve his master under a seven-year indenture, all the while learning the business of trade and commerce. But he became dissatisfied, stifled in just one more way, and he escaped his indenture, tearing up the contract, and lighting out for the adventures he still had in mind. The farm was behind him, he had left a future that might have brought him a secure career, and his prospects were uncertain. But at least he was free to pursue his own destiny.

SOLDIERING ON A WORLD STAGE

By this time, Smith was ready to meet the world, and he set his sights on becoming a soldier. He was a young man in his late teen years who had grown a great red beard, one he sported most of his adult life. However, he had a physical drawback for a would-be soldier—he was short, even among the men of his day, who were shorter generally than the average height today. But what Smith lacked in stature, he made up for in confidence and bravado. He launched his military career and his days abroad by serving in the English army in France, fighting on behalf of Dutch independence from Catholic Spain.

Unemployed following the war, with few prospects, Smith went back to England and studied warfare, reading texts and treatises on the subject and gaining knowledge of how to lead men and the responsibilities that come with such leadership. All things military consumed him.

By 1600, which marked his twentieth birthday, Smith went to Holland, yet found no work as a soldier. He then set his eyes on his military possibilities in eastern Europe. His journey eastward took him through France and Italy, where he took in the local sights much as a tourist. He traveled through the eastern Mediterranean, working off his passage on board a merchant ship, landing in Egypt. Finally, Smith reached Vienna, where he ended up hiring himself out to the Holy Roman emperor Rudolf II. Rudolf's Catholic empire was in a conflict with the Ottoman Empire of the Turks, who were threatening central and eastern Europe. This conflict would become known as the Long War. Although Smith was a Protestant, he agreed to fight for Rudolf, desperate to make himself into the soldier he longed to become.

In 1602, Smith joined a battalion led by a military leader named Zsigmond Báthory, who marched his army straight into the conflict in Transylvania. These were days of intense military activity for Smith; he became further adept with weaponry, including handguns, battle-axes, lances, and swords. His experiences included battles at sea and on land. He appears to have brought to his military encounters a certain level of natural instinct. He was brave to a fault and strong in a fight. His prowess led to Smith receiving a command of a cavalry unit of 250 men, who subsequently laid siege to a walled city. Smith could not know then, of course, that these years as a mercenary were preparing him for the extraordinary challenges he would meet in the wild and savage backcountry of North America.

It was during this field of action, according to Smith's autobiography, that he first proved himself as a man of war. During a siege on the front lines, as both armies watched, the intrepid Englishman managed to kill three Turkish opponents, each in turn, in

SMITH'S QUESTIONABLE DUEL

At times in his autobiography, John Smith presents himself as little more than a braggart. Sometimes his claims concerning himself are either difficult to corroborate or they are downright fabrications. One such claim has Smith the soldier engaging in a duel that sounds strikingly similar to the biblical story of David and Goliath.

While serving as a mercenary in eastern Europe against the Ottoman Turks, Smith accepted a challenge issued by the enemy, a Turkish leader named Turbashaw. The Turkish commander suggested to Smith's commander that he send his best fighter out to engage Turbashaw's best soldier and fight a duel to the death. Smith soon engaged his Turkish opponent. Rather than throw a stone from a sling like the biblical David, Smith and his opponent mounted horses and rode toward one another, each lowering a wooden lance at the other. When the two men came into contact range, Smith managed to pierce his enemy with his lance. The soldier fell backward off his horse, dead. The tough English mercenary then dismounted his steed, pulled out his sword, and proceeded to cut off his enemy's head, which he then presented to his commander, who, according to historian Bradford Smith, "kindly accepted it." Smith then proceeded to engage two other Turkish challengers and managed to beat each one, beheading them both.

Despite Smith's claims, history is uncertain whether he actually killed three Turkish challengers in back-to-back encounters. Nevertheless, when he finally returned from his eastern European exploits to England in 1604, he had gathered for himself enough of a reputation as an experienced soldier for the Virginia Company to hire him on as their military leader.

a prearranged challenge issued by the enemy leader. After defeating each in combat, as Smith claimed in his later writings, he cut off their heads with a sword. For his skill and repeated acts of bravery, Smith was awarded a coat of arms from the king of Poland, as well as a captain's rank, a pension, and recognition as an English gentleman. (His coat of arms included the heads of his three Turkish victims.) The days of John Smith on a farm must have seemed distant, indeed.

COMPASSION FOR THE CAPTAIN

Despite his success, Smith's luck did not hold out forever. Soon afterward, he was wounded during a battle against the Tartars and then captured. Several captives, Smith included, were delivered to the old medieval town of Axiopolis (today the city is known as Cernavodă, Romania), where the English captive was placed on the auction block. Smith later described his situation as "sold for slaves, like beasts in a market-place; where every merchant, viewing their limbs and wounds, caused other slaves to struggle with them, to try their strength." Smith's wounds did not keep him from being purchased by a slaver who represented a client. Soon, the captured mercenary found himself in the ancient city of Constantinople (present-day Istanbul).

The client for whom the war-weary John Smith had been purchased turned out to be a young girl who decided to send him on to her brother. The brother, a military commander who was stationed close to the Black Sea, immediately set about making certain the captured soldier would not prove to be a problem. He ordered one of his servants to strip Smith of his clothes, then shave his head and burgeoning red beard. Smith was then fitted with "a great ring of iron, with a long stalk bowed like a sickle, riveted about his neck." The

How he flew BONNYMVLGRO Chap. 7.

John Smith's combat against the third Turk is depicted in this illustration. Smith's military background turned out to be critical to the safety and success of the Jamestown colony.

great warrior who had defeated three Turks in a busy day of battling and beheading was reduced to nothing more than an abused slave, far from friends and home.

Restrained and humiliated, Smith was forced to work on a farm, the very existence he had left behind years earlier in England. But the tenacious Englishman would not remain in such circumstances for long. Within just a few months, he managed to kill his captor and escape. By his own words, he "beat out [his master's] brains with his threshing bat." Then, he dressed in his victim's clothing and set out on an escape to the west.

He found a caravan road to Astrakhan, a city in southern Russia, situated along the banks of the Volga River, near the Caspian Sea. Eventually, he made his way to Prague, the Holy Roman Empire's capital city. From there, he continued, done with fighting in eastern Europe, completing a hazardous, intrepid journey across Germany and France, then to Spain and North Africa. Along the Barbary Coast of Morocco, he encountered French pirates, who agreed to take him on as a crewman. His adventures continued, including one more continental fight, this time against the Spanish, that almost ended in capture by Spaniards, plus a gunpowder explosion on board the pirate ship. Finally, he made his way home to England during the winter of 1604–1605.

In 1606, Smith, still restless and again unemployed, eventually heard of a plan by London merchants to plant an English colony in America, in the region of the Chesapeake Bay that had already been named for England's beloved monarch, Elizabeth I, the "Virgin Queen." (Elizabeth had died in 1603, while Smith was fighting his way across eastern Europe. A new monarch, James I, who was also the king of Scotland, had ascended to the throne.) While in London, Smith had made himself conspicuous, telling his tales of his military adventures and extraordinary experiences.

He had heard of Virginia even before hearing of the planned colonizing effort. It is possible he had attended the Blackfriars Theater, where he could have sat or stood in the audience and seen a performance of a new production, *Eastward Hoe,* in which Virginia was described "as pleasant a country as ever the sun shined on." Such a claim might have meant something to the restless Smith, who, while only in his mid-twenties, had seen many countries and a good part of the Western world. As an avid reader, he was likely familiar with a poem by English poet Michael Drayton that also extolled the virtues of Virginia: "To get the pearl and gold / And ours to hold / VIRGINIA / Earth's only paradise." This land in America—Virginia—was beginning to captivate the imagination of Captain John Smith.

2

The New World

History is uncertain just exactly how and from whom John Smith heard about the planned venture to establish an English toehold in Virginia. What is known is that Smith and two other men recruited a variety of individuals to invest in the planned colony. They obtained the support of the Crown, which lured wealthy and powerful merchants expecting to see repayment in the form of New World natural resources such as fish, fur, and timber.

Two groups were formed: the Virginia Company of Plymouth, whose land grant was bounded by the latitudes 38° and 45° north (the territory from today's Maine south to Chesapeake Bay); and the Virginia Company of London, which received rights to colonize between latitudes 34° and 41° north (from modern-day North Carolina and to the mouth of the Hudson River).

On December 10, 1606, the ships, crew, and colonists were ready to set sail. The ship's captain was the de facto leader of the colony once they made landfall in Virginia. Captain Christopher Newport was a skilled mariner who had been to America many times, including as part of the rescue expedition sent to Roanoke Island in 1590.

Upon arrival in the New World in the spring of 1607, the colonists settled on land situated along the northern banks of the James River, with a narrow causeway connecting it to the mainland. They called the settlement Jamestown. These lands were home to a cultural group of Indians called the Algonquian. The Indians in the Tidewater region of the Chesapeake belonged to dozens of tribes all scattered about, so that Jamestown was virtually surrounded, with Indians living in every direction from the English settlement.

ENGLISH DIPLOMACY

The English exploring party progressed up the river. Two days out, they encountered a party of eight Indians in a canoe. One of them seemed especially astute, as well as friendly. Named Navirans, he communicated with the men in signs and even drew a map of the river when given pen and ink. He told the English he would serve as their guide up the river. He then led the party to his village, where the colonists met his brother-in-law, Chief Arahatec. The chief's people fed the Englishmen a good meal of roasted deer meat, mulberries, beans, and corn cakes. The English met with a visiting chief from another village, whom they gave small gifts such as penny knives, scissors, and beads. The locals called him Powhatan, but he was not the same powerful Powhatan, father of Pocahontas, whom Smith would meet early the following year. Later in their expedition, the colonists reached this "lesser" Powhatan's village, located on a high hill flanked by fields of corn, beans, peas, and pumpkins. That site was situated just a couple of miles downriver from today's site of

Richmond, Virginia. After meeting with these Indians, the men pressed on, but they soon arrived at a waterfall, which ended their voyage up the waters of the James River.

Before leaving the region, they erected a cross bearing the name of King James, even as they claimed the land in his name. On their return, the Englishmen stopped by one of the villages in which they had stayed a few days earlier. There, they demonstrated their guns, which seemed to frighten as well as impress Chief Arahatec.

A few days into their journey, Navirans, who had remained with them for several days and guided them along the river, suddenly announced he would go no farther down the river with the English. This caused some immediate concern—Smith wrote it gave "just cause of jealousy [suspicion]"—which caused the party to hurry back to Jamestown, where they found their suspicion warranted. In their absence, the Jamestown settlement had been attacked by several hundred Indians. With no real palisade to protect them, the English had suffered many arrows, which had ripped their tents, wounded more than a dozen men, and killed two. Only a broadside fired from one of the ships had caused the Indians to break off their attack and flee. Suddenly, Smith's earlier concerns about the settlement's vulnerability had proved correct. It was determined the settlers should build a fort and arm their men.

SMITH'S IMPORTANCE INCREASES

Smith was quickly adapting to his new environment. As a soldier, he had found himself over the previous decade or so in various exotic worlds, where cultural practices, societies, and even religions varied widely from one another. Here, in the New World, Smith was soon making the transition from life in England to life on the American frontier. He was already proving to be a master of resourcefulness. He

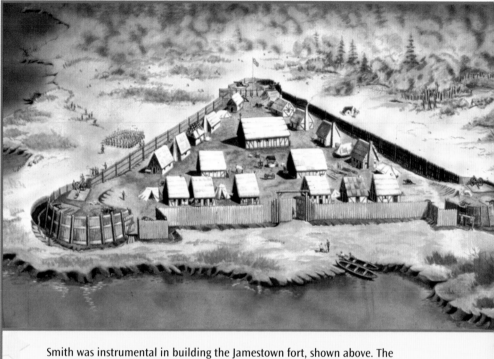

Smith was instrumental in building the Jamestown fort, shown above. The structure kept the colonists safe from attacks by Indians and other Europeans.

had demonstrated such on Newport's second voyage up the James. Now that a palisade of logs was needed to protect the community, Smith's knowledge of fortification immediately came into play. No one among the party of colonists had seen more types of forts and military structures than John Smith.

The fort was three-sided, a defensive triangle of standing logs at about 8 feet (2.4 meters) in height. At intervals, loopholes were cut in the fort's walls to allow armed defenders to fire their weapons at either Indian or Spaniard. At each of the three corners, a crescent-shaped bulwark was built and mounted with four or five small cannons. Two of the corner gun emplacements faced out toward the river, as many of the English still feared discovery by their European enemies, the Spanish, more than the immediate threat of the Indians.

PROBLEMS ABOUND

By the fall of 1607, the colonists were struggling with disease, in part due to the location of their settlement. As they were situated on low-lying, almost swampy land, mosquitoes were a constant problem. Men contracted malaria without understanding that the tiny insects were the cause. In addition, the groundwater became polluted. As the ground was saturated, the water mingled with human waste, which caused typhoid and dysentery among the men, killing some. Historian Giles Milton notes that one of the colonists wrote of the water: "Our drinke [was] cold water taken out of the river, which was at floud [high tide] verie salt [and] at a low tide full of slime and filth, which was the destruction of many of our men."

Additionally, food was scarce. The colonists had to rely on a common cooking pot and its unappetizing contents. One description went as follows: "[It] was halfe a pinte of wheat and as much barly boyled with water for a man a day, and this having fryed some 26 weeks in the ship's hold, contained as many wormes as graines." As for the hardened Captain Smith, who had faced wretched army food on more than one occasion, he hardly flinched while eating half-cooked, wormy barley gruel. But many in the settlement could not stand such fare, and sickness spread. Death stalked the colonists, and come August, scarcely a day passed without the death of one of their number, creating a scattering of grave sites around the island. By September 10, half the colony was dead. Even the stalwart Smith became ill for a time and thought he might die. Only a continuing supply of sturgeon fished from the river, some of them as long as 7 feet (2 m), kept the colony from completely dying out. That, and a gift of corn from some Indians and the arrival of north-bound waterfowl on the river, including, noted Smith, "swans, geese, duckes and cranes."

EXPLORING THE REGION

The new food sources helped the remaining colonists to survive into the fall of 1607. Smith later wrote: "God so changed the hearts of the salvages [savages] that they brought such plenty of their fruits and provision as no man wanted." But food for a day or a week did not solve the overall and constant needs of the colonists. The leadership of the settlement was in the hands of Captain John Ratcliffe—one of the seven men chosen by company officials to a council directing the colony—who appointed Smith as the colony's chief merchant. This meant it was up to Smith to keep the colony supplied with food. To that end, he immediately organized a food-finding expedition, taking several of the men who were well enough to travel and heading off into the interior. Armed with the usual trinkets, hatchets, and such, he was soon bartering with Indians for great quantities of food, including venison, corn, and oysters. (In one version of Smith's later writings, he claimed he and his six or seven comrades stole an effigy, or religious figure of some sort, then threatened to keep it unless the Native Americans filled his boat with food, to the tune of 16 bushels of corn.)

September became October, then November, and the colony seemed fairly secure, for the moment at least. Food could never be taken for granted, nor good relations with the Indians. By early November, the leadership decided to dispatch Captain Smith into the Virginia interior to meet with the leader of the Powhatan Confederacy, Powhatan himself. With such earlier examples of

AN UNFORTUNATE FATE

One of the men Smith included in his party on November 9, 1607, was a colonist named George Cassen. When Smith left the barge and continued up the narrowing Chickahominy in a canoe, he ordered those he left behind to wait for him. He also said that "none should goe a shore till his returne." Cassen did not take Smith's warning seriously. The captain had not left them long before Cassen went ashore, where he was immediately grabbed by Indians hiding in the undergrowth. They began to question him, asking his purpose for being in their territory, with the captured colonist refusing to tell them anything. His stubbornness would cost him.

The Indian warriors stripped off his clothes and tied his feet and hands with ropes. They then built a fire, as Cassen was "tyed to a tree and, with muscle-shells or reedes, the executioner cutteth of his joyntes one after another, ever casting what is cut off into the fier." Slowly, methodically, against the screams of the unfortunate Jamestown resident, the Indians disjointed Cassen. Several kept his fingers and toes as keepsakes after removing the skin.

They then went to work on his torso, cutting him open and removing his intestines. They used shells to remove the skin from his head and face. Finally, after Cassen had been hacked apart and cut open, the Indians gathered up coals from the fire, set them in a ring around the tree the colonist was tied to, and burned his remains.

All this happened, of course, without Smith's knowledge. By the time Cassen had been captured, having failed to heed the captain's words, Smith and his smaller party were nearly 20 miles (32 kilometers) to the north, making progress on their way to see Powhatan.

English colonizing failures as Roanoke and more recently, the Popham colony, one thing was clear: For Englishmen to survive in the New World, they had better stay on the positive side of the Indians with whom they shared land. Leaders at Jamestown were also still interested in any information local Indians might have concerning the fate of the colonists at Roanoke who had disappeared 20 years earlier.

On November 9, Smith set out in another of the colony's river craft, a small barge, along with nine colonists, including six oarsmen. It was decided the barge, also called a pinnace, would follow on the next high tide, with seven more men. Powhatan lived to the north, so Smith and his company sailed along the James for 5 miles (8 kilometers) or so to the mouth of the Chickahominy, then turned north into the wide mouth of that Virginia tributary. The virgin vegetation grew close to the river, leaving Smith to hack at tree branches with his sword. As his boat moved along, Smith worked on a map, noting each bend or turn in the river. In time, the river narrowed so that the barge could go no farther. Meeting with some local Indians, Smith bartered for one of their canoes, then continued upriver with two other colonists and a pair of Indian guides. In the meantime, the rest of his crew rowed the barge downstream, where they were to wait until Smith and his reduced party rejoined them.

With his smaller party, Captain Smith continued up the Chickahominy, even as trouble stalked his moves. In short order, he had followed a channel of the river that was soon clogged with reeds, a marshy ground that made progress difficult. Smith chose to tie up the canoe and continue on foot with one of his Indian guides. He ordered his two English companions to stay in the boat, keep a sharp eye, and keep their fuse, or match, lit (they were carrying matchlock guns) so they could fire their muskets. The men were to fire a shot if they saw any Indians.

How they tooke him prisoner in the Ooze 1607.

C. Smith bindeth a salvage to his arme fighteth with the King of Pamaunkee and all his company, and slew 3 of them.

In the midst of an expedition, Smith was taken prisoner by Indians. This engraving was printed in Smith's publication *The Generall Historie of Virginia*.

The captain had left his comrades for barely 15 minutes before he heard shouts from their direction. He knew immediately that something was wrong, for he heard no gunshot. Certain he would soon find himself in danger, Smith acted on his military instincts. He grabbed his Indian guide and tied their arms together with a garter, intending to use the warrior as a shield. But Smith was already surrounded, and the attack came swiftly. As Smith later recounted: "I was struck with an arrow on the right thigh, a mere flesh wound." Spinning round, two Indians came into his view, each with his bow drawn. Smith fired toward them with his French wheel-lock pistol, managing to get off three or four shots. Still, arrows found their marks, and Smith was hit several times, each arrow sticking in the heavy material of his buff jerkin.

During these tense minutes, with arrows flying, Smith's captive was terrified, shouting at the attackers to stop. His words must have been heard, for the armed Indians (Smith counts them as 200 strong, which had formed a circle around him) halted their assault, seemingly ready to parley with the captain. With no real bargaining power, Smith was obliged to cooperate. Under the circumstances, their terms were generous: "They demaunded my armes, the rest they saide were slaine, only me they would reserve." The claim the Indians made concerning Smith's associates back in the canoe was true. His comrades were no more.

3

Powhatan and Pocahontas

Even under such long odds, Captain Smith did not intend to give up. He made a break for the river, running as fast as he could. But the river had given way to a boggy swamp, and the more the Englishman ran, the deeper he sank, until mud reached his knees, stopping him cold in his tracks. He continued to sink farther in the mud until it was waist deep. Suddenly, he realized he might continue sinking until his entire stocky frame was underneath, a circumstance that signaled imminent death. Ironically, his only hope seemed to be the Indians themselves. He turned to his pursuers and reached toward them, having thrown down his weapons. They in turn reached for him, pulling him from the confines of the muddy morass.

SMITH MEETS POWHATAN

But Smith was only out of the mud. His fate was no more certain. The Indians looked their captive over, fascinated by the breadth of Smith's red beard, or at least the captain thought so. They took him to a campfire site where his comrades had been killed. There, the

THE NATIVE AMERICANS OF VIRGINIA

Historians estimate that the Native Americans living in close proximity to Jamestown likely numbered between 10,000 and 15,000 people, living in disconnected villages and tribal units by the hundreds. Many of these tribes had already formed an alliance by the early 1600s as part of the powerful Powhatan Confederacy. The point of such an alliance was to provide protection from their enemies. This proved, of course, a difficulty for the colonists. With so many Indians banded together, their sheer numbers would pose a constant threat. But the nations of the Powhatan Confederacy were not the only regional native populations the Englishmen might have to face. Some tribes were not a part of the Indian alliance, yet represented significant nations, including the Susquehannok, Mannahoac, and Massawomeck. Raids between these Native Americans and those belonging to the Powhatan Confederacy were commonplace.

Thus, these new European arrivals found themselves living in a complicated world in which one tribe might be friendly toward them, while another was ready to raid against them. As for the dominant nation among the Powhatan group, perhaps the Pamunkey represented the strongest, having between 500 and 600 warriors at their disposal. The Pamunkey lived close enough to the Jamestown settlement, about an easy day's travel, that they could regularly make life difficult for their new English neighbors.

captain saw the body of one man bristling with more than 20 arrows. The Indian men let Smith warm himself by the fire. Some even rubbed his limbs to restore them from the cold of the bog.

Without a weapon, Smith had to fall back on his wits. He reached into a pocket and produced an ivory compass, and the wily Englishman made certain that, no matter where he stood, the magnetized needle pointed directly at him. The Indians seemed amazed, reaching for the needle, but unable to touch it because of the glass. Smith wrote later: "Much they marveled at the playing of the fly and needle." As if teaching a science lesson, the captive soldier then began to lecture on the nature of the cosmos. The warriors listened, according to Smith, amazed, and then they set out to take him to their village.

After a journey through several Indian villages, Smith's captors finally reached Werowocomoco, the village of Powhatan. Powhatan's dominion stretched from the Roanoke River to Chesapeake Bay, an alliance named for the chief himself. The lands representing his power included those of the Pamunkey, Chickahominy, and Potomac tribes. The party had trekked as far north as the Toppahannock River, perhaps 30 miles (48 km) north of Werowocomoco. No other Indian leader within hundreds of miles could lay claim to the scope of territory ruled by Powhatan. The captain knew he was deep inside the belly of the beast.

As Smith entered Powhatan's capital, he was greeted by those who were aghast at the bedraggled captain's appearance, thinking him some sort of monster. Then, the English captive was taken to Powhatan's dwelling. Here, he was informed that the Indian leader's proper name was not Powhatan, but Wahunsonacock. As Smith was shown into the chief's house, his eyes took a moment to adjust to the dim light. There, before him, stood 200 warriors, decorated in red paint, their hair brimming with feathers. There was a royal woman whom Smith recognized as Opussoquonuske, the beautiful queen of the Appamattuck peoples. She approached with a basin of

Smith was taken to the great chief Powhatan, who sat high on a throne surrounded by his men and by women wearing beautiful pearls. It was not clear to Smith what would be done to him.

water so that Smith could wash his hands. A second woman brought him feathers with which to dry them. It was not immediately clear to Smith which of the people in the house was Powhatan.

But then, through the subdued light, he looked toward the opposite end of the longhouse. Smith later wrote of what and who he saw, describing the Indian leader "proudly lying upon a bedstead a foote high, upon tenne or twelve mattes richly hung with manie chaynes of great pearles about his necke." Powhatan appeared as regal to Smith as if he were sitting on a throne in a grand palace. Smith describes him as tall and well-formed, with gray hair and a "sower [sour] look." There were women everywhere, it seemed to the Englishman: "At his heade sat a woman, at his feete another, on each side sitting upon a matte upon the ground were [arranged] his chiefe men . . . and behinde them as many young women, each a great chaine of white beades over their shoulders. . . . [He had] such a grave and majesticall contenance, as drove me into admiration to see such state in a naked salvage."

Both men eyed one another. Powhatan was cordial and hospitable as he ordered food to be brought in so that Smith could eat. After the food came the questions, only this time not from the English captain, but from the great chief. *Why have you and your people come here?* The wily Smith answered without answering. He made up a story, saying that the ship he and his fellow Englishmen were sailing on had fought a sea battle against the Spanish and had been driven into the region of the Chesapeake and that the settlement they had built was only temporary. *Why are you encroaching so far to the north, on my land, if you are not going to stay here?* Smith explained that the English were searching for a route to the west, to the South Sea (Pacific Ocean). He also explained that a member of the English colony had been killed by Monacan Indians from the mountains to the west and that Smith was searching for them to avenge the death. These were lies, of course, but Smith was desperate to stay alive, hoping to present himself and his colleagues back at Jamestown as no threat to Powhatan and his people.

Powhatan then told his own stories, informing Smith of a great salt sea to the west beyond the Appalachian Mountains, no more than a week's journey away. He told Smith of a tribe of cannibals who lived there, the Pocoughtronack, who shaved their heads, and with whom Powhatan's people had battled. He also told of a people dressed like the Englishman, in coats and shirts, who had also arrived by ship. To whom he might have been referring, if anyone, is uncertain. Perhaps he meant the French, who had already arrived in Canada to the north and were pushing up the St. Lawrence River toward the Great Lakes. Between the two men, each had his tales to tell.

Then, in case Smith had not already been impressed with the scope of the chief's lands, Powhatan delivered a long speech describing his domain and the power he held accordingly. Smith was then invited to tell about the place where he was from. The captain was more than happy to oblige, describing the majesty of King James I and of the royal navy at his command. He went into detail, perhaps to frighten Powhatan and his warriors, describing English military might, mimicking the sound of cannons and battlefield trumpets.

As Smith bragged patriotically about England, Powhatan listened. But the Indian king was no fool. He was well aware of the struggles that had been taking place at the English settlement along the James River; of how dependent the English had been on support from him and his alliance of tribes. The settlement at Jamestown was not his first encounter with European arrivals to his shores. Of late middle age, he knew of the Roanoke Colony of 20 years ago, as well as an attempt by Spanish Jesuits who had landed along the coast of Chesapeake Bay.

As he watched and listened to Captain Smith, he had reason to doubt the Englishman's stories. Recently, he had listened to his own elders, wise old ones in his village who had prophesied to him concerning the threat of these new people. They had told him that "from the Chesapeake Bay, a nation should arise, which should dissolve and give end to his [empire]." The timing of the Jamestown colony may have doubly worried Powhatan, for his elders had told him that, after the first two European attempts to establish a presence in the region, "the third time, they themselves [the Indians] should fall into their subjection and under their conquest." To Powhatan, Jamestown represented that third attempt. For nearly eight months, he had watched, through his spies, the colony at Jamestown take root. Early on, he had sent diplomats offering friendship with the English, who delivered a promise from their great chief that there should be no hostilities between them.

Now, with this warrior of the English before him, Powhatan had a decision to make. He met with his elders, discussing what to do with Smith. Death seemed the choice. Powhatan had ordered the deaths of others before. He had two favorite means of dispatching someone—either by bashing their brains out or cooking them over an open fire. He and the elders conferred, and the choice was made: The Englishman's head would be crushed. He and his encroaching people must be stopped.

Suddenly, many warriors leaped forward, taking Smith in their hands as he struggled against them. Then, one of the most famous events in early American history may have taken place. With Smith overpowered, warriors stood ready with clubs in hand, the corners of the longhouse filled with their whoops and shouts. Out of the shadows stepped a young girl intent on changing Captain Smith's fate. The hapless Englishman recorded what happened next: "Pocahontas, the King's dearest daughter, when no intreaty could prevaile, got his [Smith's] head in her armes and laid her owne upon his to save him from death." As if from the pages of a romance novel or a modern-day movie, this young girl had boldly stepped forward and rescued her father's would-be victim from sure death.

POCAHONTAS

Who was this impetuous girl of the great chief, whose story is remembered by schoolchildren? In his writings, Captain Smith, a man of 27 years, describes her having a beauty beyond all others among her people. She is described as well proportioned and fair. Her age on that fateful day in January 1608 is uncertain. She may have been 11 or 12, or perhaps as old as 13 or 14. (When she had her portrait painted in London in 1616, her age was recorded as 21.)

It appears that, among the many children of Powhatan, she was his favorite. Her name was Matoaka. But she was also known by her nickname, a special name given her because "her disposition was so lighthearted and lively." The name translated into English was something close to "Frolicsome," but the Indian name was "Pocahontas."

For some reason, in the midst of this savage scene of murder on the frontier, she had been motivated to intervene against the express will of her father. Almost immediately, seemingly due to her singular actions, Powhatan changed his mind. He reacted with apparent astonishment, sensing that the actions of Pocahontas represented a sign from the spirits that Smith should be allowed to live. Smith noted that, once the Indian girl asked that he be spared, "the Emperour was contented he should live to make him hatchets, and her bells, beads, and copper; for they thought him as well of all occupations as themselves." Not only was Smith to keep his brains inside his head after all, but Powhatan immediately adopted him. The only stipulation was that the English captain was to "goe to Jamestown to send him [Powhatan] two great gunnes and a grindstone, for which he would give him [Smith] the Country of Capahowosick, and for ever

Powhatan's daughter Pocahontas saved John Smith from the Indians' clubs. With this act, a strong bond was formed between the English colonist and the Indian girl.

esteeme him as his sonne." What a turn of events, and all in almost no time flat.

What exactly had happened? Was this young girl infatuated with this English stranger who had been delivered into her father's presence? Or was something else taking place that Smith might not have realized at the time? There are more questions than answers. But the captain's life was spared, and Smith was soon initiated into the nation of Powhatan. The ceremony took place two days later, when the Englishman was led into a longhouse located in the nearby woods and left by himself to sit in front of a fire. Then, out from behind a hanging mat emerged Powhatan and 200 of his warriors, with all their faces painted black, whooping about the room. Smith was then informed he was Powhatan's son and friend, a member of his nation. Smith was even given a new name—Nantaquoud. Then, the Indian chief sent the captain to Jamestown in the escort of a dozen of his warriors, with two carrying a large quantity of bread, another serving as his personal bodyguard, and another carrying the captain's coat. This was an entirely different escort than the one that had delivered him to Werowocomoco.

4

Exploring the Unknown

By the time Smith returned to Jamestown, he had been absent for more than three weeks. There were those who were angry at his long absence; others questioned his version of events.

It became commonplace for Native Americans to visit the fort from time to time, primarily for trade. One regular Indian visitor to Jamestown was Pocahontas. She made deliveries of food to the colonists and seemed to enjoy her time among the Englishmen, particularly the settlement's children.

It appears her primary motive for visiting Jamestown, however, was Captain Smith. The visits were undoubtedly important to Smith, as well. He wanted to hone his skills at the Indian tongue and probably hoped that, through hospitality to Powhatan's favorite daughter, the Indian king might remain friendly to the English colonists.

Events moved forward in Jamestown following Smith's return. The 38 men still left alive were excited by the January 2 return of Captain Newport and his shipload of fresh supplies, which included such exotic foods as bananas and pineapples from the Caribbean, plus a few colorful parrots for the enjoyment of the colonists. The ship also delivered new colonists, all men, approximately 100 in number, including 33 gentlemen, 21 laborers, and an assortment of craftsmen, everyone from a tailor to a gunsmith to a goldsmith to a tobacco pipe maker.

A CRUSHING LOSS

But new tragedy struck soon after Smith's return. A fire swept through Jamestown, burning several thatch-roofed buildings. Most of the colonists' clothing and personal items were gone. Fortunately, most of the new supplies had not yet been off-loaded. This marked the beginning of a litany of tragedies that would befall the colony over the following six months. By the summer of 1608, two out of three colonists would be dead, the president of the council would be under arrest, another council member would be shot, and a third close to hanging.

Perhaps the fire led Captain Newport to take his next step, one that would include Captain Smith directly. With the colony's resources at a near total loss, Newport decided to lead a new expedition in the pinnace and the barge to visit Powhatan. He believed that the discovery of gold would ultimately rescue the colony (he had just brought two refiners and two goldsmiths on board his ship) and that the Indians likely knew where such gold deposits could be found. Soon, a party of three dozen men or so, including Newport, Smith, and Ratcliffe, were on their way to visit Werowocomoco.

Settlers trade with local Indians at the Jamestown fort. Such trade helped relations between the two groups and also helped the colonists survive.

TO POWHATAN'S VILLAGE

The boats and their crews made their way to the Indian leader's village, not knowing whether Powhatan would greet them as friend or foe. When they came within a short distance of Werowocomoco, Smith and half the party set out on foot for the village, where they were soon greeted by hundreds of Powhatan's people.

The chief welcomed the English captain he had recently adopted but asked him about the cannons he had requested. When Smith explained the Indians had chosen not to haul the two guns he had procured for them, the old chief only laughed and suggested that, next time, they should be offered smaller weapons, "some of less burthen." Smith gave gifts to his "father" Powhatan, including a suit of clothes dyed scarlet, a white greyhound, and a hat. In return, the

Indian king announced "a perpetuall league and friendship" with his English neighbors.

The two men continued their talks, as Smith reminded Powhatan that he had promised lands for the English. The Indian leader shrewdly suggested that, first, the English should surrender their weapons. The captain countered that such a thing was what "our enemies desired, but never our friends." As an alternative sign of friendship, the captain proposed that the two parties exchange individuals. Two young men were chosen, including an Indian named Namontack and a 13-year-old English boy named Thomas Savage, who must have been either thrilled or frightened at the prospect. All this pleased Powhatan, who declared Smith to be a werowance, or chief, even as he stated that all the Englishmen in his village were now members of his family.

Following this first day of diplomacy and posturing, the two sides got down to business. Trade was important to both the English and the Indians. Each had something the other needed or valued. Powhatan had corn and other foods, while the colonists had something highly prized by the American Indians they were bargaining with—English copper. Before the transactions were completed, Smith used deceit to trade a few bags of glass beads (the blue ones were new to Powhatan, and he immediately placed great value on them) for 200 to 300 bushels of corn from Powhatan by appealing to his vanity. He told the proud chief that such "jewels" were prized by the highest monarchs in Europe. Everyone seemed satisfied with the outcome of the day's bargaining, and it was all followed with a great feast and speeches and "playng, dauncing, and delight."

After several days in Powhatan's village, the English loaded up their food stores, with Newport in the pinnace and Smith manning the barge. The meetings with Powhatan had gone well, yet Newport may have overstayed his time in the colony. He did not leave

(continues on page 40)

DISCOVERING JAMESTOWN AND WEROWOCOMOCO

More than 400 years have passed since the English established their toehold in America, which they called Fort James or Jamestown. Over the years, the actual site of the fort fell into disrepair and was abandoned, especially as the number of colonists became too many for all to remain inside the fort. By the nineteenth century, no one was certain of the exact location of the old fort. It would remain for archaeologists in the twentieth century to relocate the place that time had long since covered over.

Excavations of the Jamestown Rediscovery Project began in the spring of 1994 under the direction of archaeologist Dr. Bill Kelso. The Association for the Preservation of Virginia Antiquities sponsored the project. The search for the former colonial site was a challenge since the conventional wisdom was that the river had eaten away the shoreline of the fort's island location. If so, that would mean the fort site was actually under the waters of the James River.

Kelso chose an area for digging that had not been unearthed before. He picked his location based on the only remaining aboveground building left from the original Jamestown—a church tower. Kelso knew, from the descriptions of the fort, that the church itself had been in the midst of the fort. He selected high ground nearby and began digging. After a little more than two years, Kelso and his team of diggers located the fort's foundations. Systematic digging over the years since has revealed 87 percent of the original site, with the remaining portion of the triangular fort—basically one of the bulwark corners—underwater.

Later excavations revealed over 1 million artifacts, including musket balls, clay pipe stems, pottery, weapons, tools, coins, fish hooks, pieces of glass, and many other common, everyday items. One intriguing find is a small, lead luggage tag, about 1 by 2 inches (2.5 by 5 centimeters), stamped with its destination— "YAMESTOWNE." (The Y is the Latin J.)

Bones excavated include those of thousands of fish, especially large sturgeons that must have been extremely plentiful. Other bones include those of dolphins and sharks, apparently eaten by the colonists. Trade items have been unearthed, including shell beads and glass beads. Copper, highly prized by the local Native Americans as a trade good, has also been found.

Other interesting finds include burial sites and the skeletal remains of 85 early colonists. One of the most intriguing skeletons, from a site within the fort, was that of a teenaged boy, along with an arrowhead from a leg wound. In Smith's writings, he refers to the first Indian attack at Jamestown, during which a boy was killed by an arrow.

Less than 10 years after the Jamestown Rediscovery Project began, other archaeologists went to work on excavations in search of the site of Powhatan's village, Werowocomoco. Historians had generally identified a site near the north bank of the York River in modern-day Gloucester County as the Indian village, but in 2002–2003, an archaeological survey and later diggings revealed a more likely site to the west, on Purtan Bay. (Archaeologist Daniel Mouer, from Virginia Commonwealth University, actually identified the site in 1977.) Further excavations on a 50-acre (20-hectare) site have unearthed many artifacts dating to the seventeenth century, as well as a complex of earthworks that date back to approximately the year 1400. In 2006, the Werowocomoco Archaeological Site was added to the National Register of Historic Places.

The digging at the assumed Werowocomoco site has been directed by two local archaeologists, Thane Harpole and David Brown. In 2004, the Werowocomoco Research Group unearthed two curving ditches, each more than 200 feet (61 m) in length, situated about 1,000 feet (305 m) from the Pamunkey River. Continued work at the site may ultimately reveal a D-shaped construction that shows up on a map of Werowocomoco drawn by John Smith.

(continued from page 37)

Jamestown until April, which meant that each week he stayed, his own crewmen were consuming supplies intended for the colonists. In addition, Newport's men were forcing those in Jamestown to pay dearly for food and other items provided by the company, supplies that should have been handed out freely to the settlers. Also, too many men were spending their time doing nothing, Smith later wrote, but "dig gold, wash gold, refine gold, loade gold." The captain disapproved of it all, for, as one colonist noted: "Never any thing did more torment him then to see all necessary business neglected, to fraught such a drunken ship with so much guilded durt [gilded dirt]." As Newport departed, his ship was filled with the New World diggings the colonists had unearthed—ore they hoped contained gold.

AT THE FORT

The days were turning warm, and some of the men in Jamestown were busy rebuilding the settlement following the fire, while others worked planting spring crops in the nearby fields. Although overall Indian relations were good, some Indians were making trouble from time to time by approaching the fort and then stealing any tools or weapons they could get their hands on. On one occasion, while Captain Smith and a comrade were at work in a cornfield, two Indians approached, threatening the Englishmen. When they followed Smith into the fort, he had them captured, along with other Indians who were loitering about. Then, one of them admitted that there was a plot to attack the fort when Captain Newport returned. Exposed and held by the English, the Indians had no choice but to return the tools they had taken. (It is uncertain whether their story was actually true.)

Another Indian soon showed up at Jamestown, as well. Powhatan sent Pocahontas as his representative to ask for the release of the captured Indians. The old chief believed Smith had a soft spot for his daughter, and he may well have been correct. Smith did write about how attractive she appeared to him. In short order, Smith convinced the council to turn the four men over to Pocahontas, "in regard of her fathers kindness in sending her." That the Indian emperor had sent his young daughter, even though he had sons, gives an indication of how important she was to him as a spokesperson, despite her young age.

A SUMMER OF EXPLORATION

On June 2, Captain Smith set out to explore the eastern shore of the Chesapeake. He and 14 companions, including a doctor, carpenter, blacksmith, fisherman, fishmonger, tailor, laborer, and fellow soldier, cramped into a 40-foot (12-m) barge. Smith took along some water, bread, and dried meat, but hardly enough for a seven-week mission. Intending to make the most of his expedition, he brought along a notebook, compass, and probably a small quadrant to aid in any mapmaking (it would give him a reading for latitude).

Their explorations opened up new sights and lands to Smith and his men. They continued examining local river mouths and spotted islands that the captain wanted to explore, which were likely Watts and Tangier islands. They reached new Indian villages, and violence erupted as they entered the Nanticoke River, where warriors ran along the riverbank, firing volleys of arrows at the barge and crew. Smith ordered muskets fired, which wounded some of the Indians. When the barge reached the local village, Smith found it abandoned. He chose to leave some trade goods, including copper, beads, bells, and mirrors. The following day, Smith and his men encountered hundreds of Indians along the shores belonging to the Nanticoke nation. Trade soon opened. Smith noted the Nanticoke had good furs to trade. Questioning them about where the furs might have come from, the Nanticoke told him of the great village far to

Explorations undertaken by Smith and other colonists taught them about local resources and introduced them to various regional Indian tribes.

the north of the Massawomeck. Smith was extremely interested. Furs were highly prized back in England.

Smith and his men continued. They covered 100 miles (161 km) over the next two days, finding no Indians. The English could not have known that local Indians had been pushed out of the region by the Massawomeck and Susquehannok nations to the north. After two weeks of exploring, several of Smith's men were ready for the voyage to end, complaining of the wet, the weather, and their seasickness. But Smith would have none of it, reminding them they would be shamed to return to Jamestown prematurely.

MEETING THE SUSQUEHANNOK

Once back in Chesapeake Bay, Smith continued north for only a few more miles, reaching Gunpowder River. Rather than continue farther, he sent a pair of local Indians north to find the Susquehannok and ask them to come south and meet with the English party. A few days later, a party of 50 or so Susquehannok did reach the barge, their canoes filled with deer meat, baskets, shields, bows, arrows, and smoking pipes with stems a yard long. These were some of the largest Indians the English had seen yet. They were not Algonquian stock like the nations the English in Jamestown were accustomed to. These were Iroquois peoples who knew of Powhatan only by name. Yet, while the English may have been new to these northern tribesmen, they were accustomed to Europeans, as they carried French hatchets from trading in Canada. The Susquehannok tried to make a singular impression on the English, especially their leader. Smith soon found himself covered in a large, painted bearskin and a white bead necklace he thought might weigh 7 pounds (3 kilograms). Other gifts were placed at his feet. Perhaps the gifts' purpose was clear when the Susquehannok asked Smith to ally with them against the Massawomeck. The captain begged off, though he promised to return the next year.

UP THE PATAWOMECK

On June 15, the party turned south back into familiar waters. The barge soon floated close to the site of modern-day Annapolis, Maryland, and continued, making 100 miles (161 km) of progress before nightfall, landing at the mouth of the Patawomeck (Potomac) River. It was here that Smith and his men left Chesapeake Bay for their longest river exploration. The captain likely had in mind, given the wide mouth of the river, the possibility that ahead of them lay the Northwest Passage, the long-illusive water route across North America to the Orient.

But 30 miles (48 km) up the river, they were immediately put upon by a party of 300 to 400 Indian warriors who, Smith noted, came out from behind trees "so strangely paynted, grimed and disguised, shouting, yelling, and crying as so many spirits from hell could not have shewed more terrible." Smith and his men fired warning shots along the surface of the river, the bullets skipping off the water and the echoing concussion frightening the Indians so that they dropped their bows and arrows. Interviewing the disarmed warriors, Smith believed that the attack had been ordered by Powhatan himself, who may have fallen into a plot with some of those back in Jamestown who were opposed to Smith. Some had recently tried to leave the fort on Newport's departing ship, but Smith had forced them to "stay in their country against their wills."

The Englishmen continued in their explorations of one of Virginia's foremost rivers today, the Potomac. They made quick progress, probably traveling as far as the river's Great Falls, approximately 20 miles (32 km) from today's Washington, D.C. There, they were blocked from going any farther by great boulders as big as trees that were scattered about their path. Smith led his men down the river to the bay and then south, reaching the mouth of the Rappahannock River. At one site, the captain tried to mimic the Indian fishers he had seen a couple of weeks earlier, using his sword as a spear. He and others caught more fish than they could possibly eat that day. But the fishing expedition ended in almost deadly fashion for Smith, whose last catch turned out to be a stingray, which thrust its barbed tail into the captain's wrist, sending deadly poison through his arm and shoulder. The swelling was so bad that everyone, including Smith, thought he would surely die, and the captain ordered his grave to be dug. Smith had chosen wisely in taking along a doctor, who cut open the wound and applied an oily medicine to the sore. Soon, the pain and swelling subsided, and Smith recovered enough to eat his share of the day's catch of fish. With that, Captain Smith decided to bring his explorations to an end.

5

Up and Down the Chesapeake

Smith and his men had been gone for most of a month, making their expedition the longest exploration throughout the region of Virginia to date. The return of the exploratory party found Jamestown in bad shape. There was much sickness in the small village. The colonists were unhappy with Ratcliffe's leadership and his insistence that they build him a large "pallace in the woods" as his personal domicile. Some approached Smith to lead a mutiny and take over as leader. Exactly what happened is unclear, but it seems that the captain did remove Ratcliffe, with the blessing of the council.

Smith waited only a few days to set off on his second reconnaissance of the summer. He chose 12 men to accompany him this time, including 9 of his previous comrades. On Sunday, July 24, the faithful boat made

JOHN SMITH'S MANY LANGUAGES

When Europeans landed in the New World, they faced many challenges. One difficult aspect of settling in a strange land was trying to communicate with the native populations, all of whom spoke their own special language, or dialect. The English who landed and settled in the Virginia Tidewater region at Jamestown had to learn these languages quickly if they were going to have any meaningful exchange with the Indians, including conducting trade.

John Smith came to the New World with several languages under his belt. His years as a soldier of fortune across the length of Europe had given him opportunity to learn tongues that might have been foreign to the average Englishman. It appears he spoke a basic form of French, as well as Dutch and Italian. It is likely that he also spoke more than one regional central or eastern European language. Once in the New World, the captain became one of the colony's best speakers of various native Algonquian dialects.

its way down the James River once again. By July 25, the party reached the village of Kecoughtan, situated at the mouth of the James River. Facing a northerly wind, the men sat tight for a few days before trying to sail north. Captain Smith took time to demonstrate something new to the Indians—fireworks. He shot off several rockets that went spiraling into the sky in a stream of sparks and flame. Such things amazed the local Indians and served as a reminder to them that the English had powers and weapons they did not.

Once the winds died down, Smith and his party set out into Chesapeake Bay to the mouth of the Rappahannock. Soon, they reached the Patapsco River, nearly the farthest northern point of the

His journals include words and phrases he had learned. One of his earliest key phrases was the Algonquian sentence "*ka ka torawincs yowo*," which translates as "What call you this?" Pointing to something he wanted to learn the name of became a common means of learning Indian words. He learned the Indian name for "shoe" was *moccasin*; that *pokatawer* meant "fire," and that "water" was *suckhanna*. The Indian word for "arrows" was *attonce*. When sorting out who were the friends of the English and who were the enemies, the words *wingapoh* or *netoppew* identified the former, while those in opposition were the *marrapough*. When engaging in trade or other activities with native populations, it was good to know one's numbers. Smith learned that the numbers "one," "two," and "three" were *necut, ningh, nuss,* and so on, up to the Algonquian word for "one thousand," which was *necutweunquaough*. The English needed to know the Indian names for common trade goods as well, so Smith committed to memory such words as *tomahacks* for "axes," *pamesacks* for "knives," *mattassin* for "copper," and *pawcussacks* for "guns."

previous trip. By July 30, they were exploring new territory. But sickness slowed their progress. Some seemed close to death. Then, matters turned even more serious, as Smith's party encountered a large number of Massawomeck Indians approaching in canoes. The captain had sought these Indians on his first expedition but had failed. Now, they had found him.

With most of his men sick and a large party of Massawomeck bearing down on the barge, Captain Smith had to act quickly. To fool the Indians into thinking the English were stronger in number than they were, he had every man's hat placed on a stick and lined up along the side of the barge. Between his five healthy comrades, each held two muskets toward the onrushing canoes. The device was simple, but effective. The Indians turned around, convinced their enemy was too strong. Yet Smith approached his would-be enemy, guiding the barge closer to shore. Once the Indians realized the English were not intending to harm them, the usual round of trade opened. Before the bargaining was over, Smith and company left with their boat filled with food, bows, arrows, wooden shields, clubs, and bearskins. Although the captain expected to sit down with the Massawomeck the following morning, come dawn, they had vanished.

That day, Smith and his men came under attack again, this time by Tockwough Indians, after setting out for the eastern shore. Smith told these people of his victory over the Massawomeck the day before. This seemed to impress the warriors enough to take the Englishmen to their village. There, the Englishmen discovered the Tockwough already owned an abundance of trade goods, including hatchets and knives, which they said they had received trading with the Susquehannok. The Tockwough also told Smith that the Susquehannok lived on a river beyond the bay, which led the imaginative captain to hope they might be speaking of a route to the Pacific Ocean, the elusive Northwest Passage.

Smith soon set out northward, still intent on making contact with the Susquehannok. He did not have to wait long. Within a few days, the Susquehannok found him and brought gifts to the English captain, such as venison, tobacco pipes, and bows and arrows, as well as great strings of beads. They must have already heard of Smith, for they begged him to become "their Governour and Protector . . . to defend and revenge them of the Massawomeks." As they entreated the captain, some of the Indian men rubbed his neck in a ritual common to them to convince him to lead them. Smith had been offered this honor by other Indians, but he was not interested in leading them unless it was to the advantage of the English colony he represented. Of course, this interpretation of the actions of these

Maſſaw-omecks

Maſſawomeck

Signification of theſe markes,
To the croſſes hath bin diſcouerd
what beyond is by relation ✠
Kings howſes 2 ▨
Ordinary howſes 2 o

NIA

Cepowig

✠ Blands C:

ownes date

The Saſque=ſahanougs
are a Gyant like peo=ple &
thus a=tyred.

Vtchowig

SL S

E

SS L H

Attaock

Teſinigh

Quadroque

This illustration of a Susquehannock warrior is a detail from a 1612 map of Virginia. According to Smith, the Susquehannock begged him to be their leader.

Indians was Smith's, which he later wrote about. He naturally could have misinterpreted their meaning completely. They may have just wanted to make an alliance of friendship.

In their awkward discussion, which necessitated several translations of languages between Susquehannok and English, the Native Americans said they knew of Powhatan but knew little about him. They carried French trade goods, which they had probably only recently received. The French had begun to settle in Quebec along the St. Lawrence River to the north only about a month earlier. The Indians also spoke of a large sea west of the mountains, but it soon became clear to the English explorers that the Native Americans were referring to a location in Canada, not the Pacific Ocean. This meant they were probably referring to one of the Great Lakes, such as Erie or Huron. After a few days, Smith and his party gave their leave of the Susquehannok. The captain was intent on returning to Jamestown in time for an important council meeting scheduled for September 10. By August 8, he and his men were on their way south. They continued to explore, choosing to examine the Rappahannock River further, since they had already collected information concerning the Susquehanna, the Potomac, and the James rivers. This river held out the last possibility of a route to the Pacific. Over the next two weeks, although the English had developed largely positive relations with local Indians, problems lay ahead.

A VIOLENT ENCOUNTER

After sailing south for a week, the English reached the mouth of the Potomac River on August 14 and began their exploration of the Rappahannock. Thirty miles (48 km) inland, they reached an Indian village they had seen before, Moraughtacund. There, they met with a chief named Mosco, whom they had encountered on their earlier exploration that summer. He was an Indian, but he appeared to be partially of European origin. He had a large beard, and Smith thought he looked Spanish or perhaps French. Mosco took the opportunity to warn Smith and his men not to visit the Rappahannock who lived farther up the river because they would kill the Englishmen. It seems the two Native American nations were fighting at the time, perhaps because the Moraughtacund peoples had recently stolen three wives of the Rappahannock chief. Smith chose not to believe Mosco, thinking he did not want the English to continue on their way and wind up trading with the Rappahannock.

But Mosco's words turned out to be prophetic. Continuing upriver, the crew on the barge encountered Rappahannock warriors on the shore who gestured for the English explorers to come closer. Smith sent a member of the crew to the riverbank as part of an exchange of "hostages," a goodwill gesture. Only when Smith's pick, a young man named Anas Todkill, reached the bank did he spot several hundred Rappahannock hiding in the tall grass. As he tried to warn Smith and the others, Todkill was captured by the Indians. A fight unfolded, with the Englishmen using the shields they had received from the Massawomeck to protect themselves from Rappahannock arrows. Smith and his party fired their muskets toward the Indians, which sent them scattering. Fortunately, Todkill managed to escape and make his way to the shore. In retaliation for the attack, the English captured the Rappahannock canoes and took them back to the village of the Moraughtacund. Yet Smith intended to return upriver.

As Smith and his men approached the region of the Rappahannock village, they readied themselves for possible attack. It came swiftly. As the colonists passed beneath a high white chalk cliff, more than three dozen Indians hid among the bushes, waiting to attack. Soon, a barrage of arrows descended on the barge, hitting the shields the men had placed along the boat's sides for protection. Smith ordered the men to fire off a round each, which ended

John Smith met Mosco and the Moraughtacund during an expedition. Smith ignored Mosco's warning about the nearby Rappahannock, who attacked the party.

the Rappahannock assault, but as the boat continued, the warriors moved upriver and jeered at the Englishmen as they passed by.

Continuing up the river, Smith's barge reached three additional villages, where he and his men were well received. A little farther upstream, the party suffered a loss as one of their members, Richard Fetherstone, who had accompanied Smith on his first voyage of discovery that summer, died. While the cause of death is uncertain, it may have been from heatstroke or the feverish effects of malaria. The barge pushed onward, and the men reached the fall line on the river, at the future site of Fredericksburg, Virginia, where they left their ship long enough to place a brass cross at the site to mark their farthest advance up yet another Virginia river. As the men scattered to collect fresh water and search for gold, Indians once again attacked, sending their arrows flying toward the barge from every direction. It was during this battle that Mosco, who had joined the English on this leg of their explorations, played a decisive role. Just as Smith had earlier fooled the Susquehannok by placing hats up and down the length of the barge, so Mosco moved around in the bushes, making as much noise as he could, leading those attacking to believe that there were more Indians helping the English than just him. This seems to have convinced the attackers to break off their assault.

The English docked their barge until nightfall, then quietly began floating back down the Rappahannock, hoping to slip by any hostile Indians. The ploy did not work. Soon, arrows were striking the shields along the sides of the barge, even though no one on the boat was hit. With few options, Smith ordered the crew to continue their trip down the river, finally dropping anchor in a wide bay, out of range of arrow shots. That morning the Mannahoac showed up along the banks nearby and indicated they no longer intended to attack by hanging their bows in the branches of trees close by. Smith soon sat down with four of the Indian nation's chiefs to discuss trading. By the time the English left them, the Mannahoac had received goods and were pleased enough with the transactions for 500 of them to begin dancing and singing as the English barge slipped down the river and out of sight.

This time, as they passed the Rappahannock encampment again, the Indians came out and made it clear they did not intend to fight. When they saw the Mannahoac bows and arrows captured by the English, they were overjoyed because the Mannahoac were their enemies. The Rappahannock called for a council with Smith, indicating they wanted to become friends with the English, even though they had attacked them just days earlier. Smith took a hard line with them, reminding the Rappahannock that they had attacked him and his men twice. Threatening to destroy their village, Smith forced them to turn over their leader's bow and arrows, then promise they would not approach him and his men with any weapons. Then, the captain met with the chief, who offered to Smith the gift of three Indian wives the Moraughtacund had taken. The capture of these women had been the source of the recent violence between the Rappahannock and the Moraughtacund. The colonists then took the barge back to the Moraughtacund to tell them of the Rappahannock chief's offer. Their chief agreed and turned the three Indian women over to Smith. As Smith was not interested in receiving any Indian women, he used them for diplomatic purposes, allowing one to remain with the Moraughtacund, another to return to the Rappahannock, and the third to be given to his faithful friend, Mosco.

All this seems unimaginable today, but the agreement meant that the two Indian nations became friends, a diplomatic coup of sorts for Captain Smith. The following day, both tribes celebrated together, 600 strong between them. Smith later wrote of each nation "promising to be our friends and to plant Corne purposely for us; and we to provide hatchets, beads, and copper for them." Even as the celebrations continued, Smith and his party loaded their boat and headed back down the river, with Indians shouting their farewells.

The next day marked the end of August, and the barge reentered Chesapeake Bay, dropping anchor at the mouth of the Piankatank, the next river to the south.

The explorations of the Piankatank were quick and without dramatic incident but were followed by a strong, harrowing thunderstorm, with Smith guided by lightning flashes as the crew rowed on into the mouth of the James River on September 4, 1608. As the settlement beckoned ahead, Captain Smith took one last jaunt up a nearby river, perhaps the Elizabeth, but the stream narrowed after only a short distance, leading Smith to take another tributary of the James, the Nansemond, where they encountered a party of Indians repairing their fishing weirs and nets. Smith handed out yet another bundle of trade trinkets, which led one more group of Indians to sing and dance, begging the Englishmen to remain with them.

Smith decided to allow some of them to board his barge before leaving, but was suspicious when they asked to keep their bows and arrows. Sure enough, the astute captain and his men, after progressing farther up the river, were attacked by 200 warriors. One of his men was shot in the sleeve and his hat, but there were no others hit. After a few shots by Smith and his men, their attackers melted away, with the whole assault reminiscent of earlier attacks that had ended with the crack of English muskets. Smith and the colonists then began hacking away at the Indians' canoes tied up on shore. Given the value of such canoes (carving out a single dugout canoe could take weeks for such Indians), these Native Americans surrendered and indicated they wanted to talk and trade. Smith extracted significant payments for their attack, demanding 400 bushels of corn and a long necklace of pearls. The goods demanded by Smith were soon produced, and Smith then returned the threatened dugouts. The English, having subdued yet one more native population, headed back up the James River. They reached Jamestown on September 7, having completed a second expedition of exploration for the summer of 1608.

While those summer river voyages of Captain Smith and his small crew were hardly epic (he had, after all, not crossed an unknown ocean or an entire continent), they were important for the men and the future of the Jamestown colony. Smith and his men had traveled more than 1,000 miles (1,609 km) on each of his expeditions that summer and made first contact with several previously unknown Indian nations. Trade had taken place, even as some fighting had occurred, but much of that violence was merely defensive. The Indians could not know with certainty what or who these strange-looking, bearded men were. Smith, naturally, wrote of his summer's exploits in glowing terms, pondering how "many ever with such small meanes as a Barge of 2 tuns . . . with twelve or sixteene men did ever discover so many fayre and navigable Rivers, subject so many severall Kings, people, and Nations, to obedience, and contribution, with so little bloodshed." He had a point. For Jamestown, he had accomplished great things.

6

Conflicts at Jamestown

When Smith returned to Jamestown, a mutiny had taken place against Ratcliffe, who had tried to reestablish his own authority. Sickness had continually dogged the settlement. Heavy rains had ruined some of the colonists' food stores. Three days after Smith's return, the annual election on September 10 took place, and Smith was elevated to the position of president. This was no surprise to many. Of the seven original members of the settlement's council, Smith was the only surviving member still in Jamestown, and most men saw him as the only true and fit leader among them. The able military leader and now successful explorer took immediately to his new role. He could not know that fall of 1608 that he would remain in Jamestown for only one more year. In the meantime, over the following months, he proved himself to be the most successful leader of the early Jamestown colony.

Smith set to work immediately. He ordered the fort to be expanded into a "five-square form" since part of the palisade was badly in need of repair. The expansion doubled the size of the fort. Houses were built and the church and storehouse repaired. Still concerned about Indian attack, Smith kept his men under military discipline, ordering them to drill daily outside the fort in a grassy area dubbed "Smithfield" after the captain. Here, the men would practice their manual of arms (weapons formations), sometimes with as many as 100 Indians watching in amazement.

A month after Smith had taken the reins of leadership, Captain Newport returned with a shipload of supplies and additional colonists, including two Englishwomen and eight Germans and Poles, some of whom were skilled glassmakers. The women—a gentlewoman and her servant—were the colony's first. As the gentlewoman was married, her 14-year-old servant girl, Anne Burras, was the only available white woman in a colony of approximately 200 men. She and one of the original 1607 colonists, John Laydon, were married before the end of the year. Newport carried the same old orders from company officials back in London. The colonists were to find gold and the Northwest Passage. (They were also to continue to look for signs or information concerning the lost Roanoke Colony.) To aid in the search, Newport delivered a dismantled barge that the colonists were to carry above the falls, assemble, then continue westward. Newport also carried special orders to organize a "crowning" ceremony for Powhatan.

Immediately, renewed clashes developed between Smith and Newport. To Smith, Newport represented a challenge to his authority and personal agenda for the settlement. He also considered the goals from London impractical. He had looked for both the gold and the westerly route and found neither. Smith also knew that the colony was still struggling along, even to survive, something that officials in London seemed to be taking for granted. He was equally opposed to the coronation plans, but he did take steps to comply. He went to visit Powhatan to ask him to come to Jamestown to receive great honors.

When the great chief warily turned the offer down, Smith and Newport were forced to take the coronation to him. The special event came off rather oddly. Fifty men from Jamestown went to Werowocomoco for the crowning of Powhatan, carrying many gifts, including a bed, bedclothes, a pitcher and basin, and the highly prized copper. The chief wore a "scarlet cloake and apparel" provided by the English. At the point when he was supposed to drop to his knees and receive his honors, he refused, uncertain what the English might do to him. After "many perswasions" he finally stooped enough to be crowned. Then, the Jamestown men discharged a celebratory volley of musket fire, which startled the king with "a horrible feare." When it was all over, the chief thanked the Englishmen by giving Newport an old pair of shoes and an old deerskin cloak. To Smith, it was all overdone. Since one goal of the ritual was for Powhatan to recognize the authority of King James I, which he probably did not understand he was doing, the whole affair seemed to the captain to be little more than a waste of time and an overindulgence of the Indian leader. If anything, the coronation had only managed to add to his personal prestige. He had forced the English to come to him and give him attention and gifts, and the whole thing had cost him only shoes and a coat.

Newport was often not present at Jamestown, as he scurried around looking for gold and silver. This left Smith the latitude to carry out his more practical goals. He sought a greater economic base for the colony, encouraging the production of such goods as naval stores, including tar and pitch, glass, soap ashes, and clapboard. In addition, Smith taught his men new skills for living in the woods. When he heard complaining or heard the men swear, he was swift to react. Smith created an odd punishment that involved keeping a daily

Captain Newport insisted on carrying out special orders to "crown" Powhatan, an honor the chief accepted with suspicion. Smith was against the empty gesture.

tally of each man's outbursts of profanity; each evening, a container of water was poured inside each man's shirt sleeve for every oath. After a while, the men stopped swearing. With each of the duties Smith placed on his men, he always led by example. There was no work he assigned that he did not also do himself.

Captain Smith was so successful in leading the Jamestown colonists that some of the men, including Ratcliffe and a small faction, became jealous. This led them to try and remove Smith from his position, but they were unsuccessful. Smith was having too much success at Jamestown for the majority of the residents to question his leadership style or his authority. By December, Captain Newport set sail for England, which suited Smith just fine. Among the items the sea captain took with him was a new map Smith had drawn up based on his explorations in the Chesapeake region the previous summer.

LEFT TO STARVE

With Captain Newport's departure, Captain Smith was only too happy to return to his previous policies, both toward the colonists and the Native Americans. He thought Powhatan had been elevated too highly by the company's coronation, so he returned to his old strong-arm tactics in getting from the Indians what he and his colonists might need to survive. The pattern was generally repeated from village to village: Smith would threaten to attack an Indian town whose people did not cooperate with the colonists and trade them food for other goods. But the Indians clearly understood how vulnerable the Jamestown colonists were. If the Indians chose to deny their neighbors such necessities as food, it was likely the colony would die out, perhaps literally by starvation. That December, the number of colonists stood close to 200, with only 30 remaining among the original arrivals. Although the death rate had dropped from 60 percent during the first year of settlement to about 20 percent, food was still a weapon the Indians might use to bring down the colony. There was generally not enough food on a regular basis in the town, since each person required approximately one pint of corn at a minimum per day just to survive.

Powhatan knew he could squeeze the colonists for more goods as they moved into their second winter in Virginia. His demands seemed endless; he requested such European items as grindstones, guns, swords, glass beads, Old Country animals such as chickens, and the prized copper. He even wanted the English to build him a house similar to the ones they had built at Jamestown, a request Smith agreed to, sending the Germans to Werowocomoco for that purpose. To a point, the English had to respond to such demands, regardless of their own threats to destroy Indian villages. Such destruction would only leave them isolated, with no place to turn to for their badly needed food. The bargains became hard-won deals for the English.

Four days after Christmas, Smith and some 50 Englishmen set out for Werowocomoco to trade for food. It was a difficult boat voyage due to bad weather, for the Pamunkey River was slushy with ice, which slowed their progress. They finally arrived on January 12, and they found Powhatan prepared to demand much for his corn—40 baskets for an equal number of swords. Smith told Powhatan he did not have that many swords to spare. To trade swords for corn meant the colonists would have fewer weapons with which to defend themselves. The captain tried to act indifferently to Powhatan, telling him the colonists could just trade with someone else instead. This may have been a part of Powhatan's plan to tip the balance of power between the colonists and his people.

But these negotiations soon became a mere backdrop to Powhatan's true intentions—to put an end to the assumed threat to himself and his people that the English represented. Even as he and Smith (along with another Englishman named John Russell) negotiated in the chief's house, orders had been given by Powhatan for his warriors to surround the hut. Smith became aware of their movement outside and told Russell that they should escape before it was too late. The two men rose and dashed out, with Smith firing a warning shot from his pistol. With this, the waiting warriors stood down as Smith and his comrade ran to the relative safety of a couple dozen Englishmen who were making their way to Powhatan's house at that very moment. With guns pointed out from their group, Captain Smith intended to make a stand if need be. But Powhatan soon assured the captain that he had merely misunderstood the presence of his warriors. They had been there only to protect the chief's corn, in case some of Smith's men wanted to steal it.

Smith put the conflict aside and concluded his deal making with Powhatan. The English would get their corn. The captain was put off dramatically by the actions taken by the Indian leader and his warriors that day. He was in no mood to compromise when the corn was delivered to his boats and the Indian men told him they could guard the colonists' guns, pistols, and swords while Smith and his men loaded their boats. The captain made it clear: You load our boats, and we'll guard ourselves. There was little trust between the Jamestown settlers and their Indian neighbors.

The bartering took so long that by the time the boats were loaded, the tide was out and the colonists were stuck in Werowocomoco for an uneasy night. Smith and Powhatan continued their charade of friendliness, but the colonists were ready for anything to happen. Their fears were warranted. Once night fell, someone came calling on Captain Smith. It was Pocahontas, whom Smith referred to as Powhatan's "dearest jewel and daughter." She had two messages for the captain—that her father was sending men with food for the evening meal and that those same men had orders to kill the Englishmen as they ate, using the colonists' own swords. Should those attackers fail, she added, Powhatan had a backup plan. He had readied a larger group of warriors against the English. She pleaded, as Smith later wrote: "Therefore if we would live shee wished us presently to be gone."

What may have motivated the young Indian princess to deliver such a warning to Captain Smith, one that clearly revealed a loyalty to the Englishman and not to her own father? Historians can only guess. Perhaps this impressionable teenaged girl was infatuated with the older Englishman (Smith had turned 29 a few days earlier).

Yet for Pocahontas to come to Smith under cover of darkness to give him such information was a significant risk. If caught, she might have had a difficult time explaining her purposes. Were she discovered, there is no certainty what fate might have befallen her.

Just as Pocahontas predicted, less than an hour later, 10 or so strong Indian men arrived with plates of venison. In the meantime, Smith had his men prepare their guns. Because most carried matchlock guns, they each had to keep a long fiber cord, or "match," lit; this was used to ignite the powder in their guns. When the Indians entered the hut where Smith and his men waited anxiously, the Indians complained of the smoke from the matches and asked the Englishmen to put them out. Smith refused. Thanks to the warning from Pocahontas, Smith and his men had managed to foil the first plot to kill them. Just to make certain, Smith had the Indian food bearers taste the venison first, in case it had been poisoned.

Then, the captain sent a message to Powhatan, stating that the English were expecting him and wanted a visit from him. It was a subtle message to the Indian leader that Smith and his men were aware of the second plan to attack them with larger numbers. The English posted guards throughout the night, but the attack never materialized. Taking advantage of the midnight tides, Smith and his men left Powhatan's village. (As for Powhatan, his own distrust of the English had led him to pack up his court of wives and children and leave his own village. He and Smith would never speak directly again.) Smith allowed another colonist named Edward Brinton to remain at Werowocomoco to hunt game birds for the Indians, but it was really a ploy to keep a loyal Englishman in the Indian capital to keep an eye on the people whom the captain felt he could not really trust.

What Smith did not know at the time was that some of his men were acting as traitors and spies. The Germans whom Smith had sent to Powhatan to build an English-style house for him had decided to turn against the English colonists. They found the Indian village to be better stocked with food than Jamestown, and they came to believe their chances of survival might be better among the Indians than under Smith's leadership. All the Germans agreed to spy for Powhatan. The Indian leader had welcomed their offer and even suggested that they slow down their progress on building his house so they could have reason to go back and forth between Werowocomoco and Jamestown for a longer period of time.

After Smith left Powhatan's village in January, a pair of the Germans went to Jamestown to ask for guns and tools on behalf of Captain Smith, who knew nothing of their plot. The whole point was to procure guns to give to Powhatan. While the Germans were in the English settlement, half a dozen additional colonists chose to join them and turn against the colony. They, too, thought their chances of making it successfully through the winter might be increased by allying with the Indians. Soon, the Germans left with a load of guns, powder, shot, and swords, all for their Indian allies. When they arrived back at Werowocomoco, it did not take Brinton long to realize what the Germans were up to. He and an English trader in the village, Richard Savage, set out to tell Captain Smith of the treachery. But they were captured by some of Powhatan's men before they could reach the captain, then placed under restraint.

C. Smith taketh the King of Pamavnkee prisoner. -1608.

Smith threatened Opechancanough, Powhatan's brother, after his party was ambushed by the local Indians.

In the meantime, Smith had gone with his men to the village of Opechancanough, Powhatan's brother, located 25 miles (40 km) up the Pamunkey River, to bargain for food. They were no better received there than they had been at Werowocomoco. There, the Indian greeting was hostile, and the Englishmen were ambushed by hundreds of Indians. When Opechancanough promised the Englishmen no harm, a doubting Smith grabbed the chief by his scalp lock and stuck a pistol in the older man's chest. Before the Englishmen left the village, the Indians filled their boat with corn and other food stuffs. The Englishmen had gained their cargo only at risk to their lives. As Smith wrote later: "Men may thinke it strange there should be such a stirre for a little corne, but had it been gold, with more ease we might have got it." Ultimately, he had emerged from the threats mounted against him and his men without any loss of life, on both sides.

7

Smith Is Replaced

Back in Jamestown, John Smith once again found the village struggling to survive. Nearly a dozen men at Jamestown had drowned when winds capsized their boat. Morale was at a new low. In addition, there were still several people in the settlement who shirked their duties, often those of the gentleman class who thought they should not have to work. Others were soldiers who saw themselves as defenders of the fort, not men to be misused with farming or fishing or mending nets. Smith responded forcefully, issuing an edict to all that is remembered even today: *He that will not worke shall not eate.* Upon his return, Smith also discovered the works of the Germans and others who had turned traitor against the colony, and he took a party of 20 armed men back to Werowocomoco to seize them. Along the way, Smith was attacked by the chief of the Paspahegh

Indians, Wowinchopunck, who was intent on killing the captain to win Powhatan's approval. Smith nearly lost his life when the two men fell into the nearby river as they wrestled in a hand-to-hand battle. The chief was trying to drown the English leader, but a pair of Smith's colleagues rescued him. Quickly recovering, the maddened Smith led an attack on the chief's village, where the English killed six or seven warriors, took prisoners, burned the town, and stole their canoes. For the moment, the march to Werowocomoco was halted, and Smith and his men returned to Jamestown, fearing reprisals from any friends of the Paspahegh.

SPRING ARRIVES

During the weeks that followed, Smith led his Jamestown colonists into the spring of the year. Work was done on the fort's defenses, and colonists planted 40 acres (16 ha) of corn close to the fort. Food was still an issue, and a new wrinkle emerged, one that threatened what food supply the colony had at hand—rats. Smith wrote that they must have arrived in the colony via the ships that docked from time to time, and they bred into the thousands, raiding barrels of corn with a voracious destruction. Had the loss of corn taken place a few months earlier, it might have spelled doom for the colony. But the captain responded by scattering his people out in smaller settlements, away from Jamestown. Smith's "divide-and-survive" strategy included sending some downriver to harvest oysters, while others went down to Chesapeake Bay to fish. Some went upriver, where scattered tribes of Indians helped feed them in exchange for copper.

Smith's efforts paid off. When one colonist, "a most craftie knave" named William Dyer, plotted to leave Jamestown by stealing the *Discovery*, one of the ships on which the settlers had sailed to Virginia. Smith was informed and the culprit punished, probably with a whipping. The captain threatened to hang anyone who schemed

Although many settlers were industrious and contributed to the success of the colony, others shirked their common duties. Here, workers shape and dry bricks for the Jamestown colony.

against the colony. His military discipline kept many in line, even if he continually struggled with some who saw no purpose in working when the colony could always get food from the Indians. Some even suggested to the captain that he trade everything—guns, swords, even the fort's cannons—to keep them supplied. Smith wrote later how his strict orders helped the colony to survive its second winter: "Such was the strange condition of some 150 that had they not been . . . forced to gather and prepare their victual [food] they would all have starved or eaten one another." (This was no self-serving analysis on his part. During the next winter [1609–1610], colonists were reduced to cannibalism.) The colony was also aided by the regular arrival of Indians, who brought wild game almost daily, including squirrels, turkeys, and venison. Through Smith's year spent leading the colony, the death rate remained very low—only 18 out of 200 colonists. Of that number, 11 had died when their boat capsized.

During the intervening months, Smith sent another party to seize the traitorous men, who were returned to Jamestown and their executions soon ordered. Before the sentence could be carried out, a ship arrived at Jamestown on July 9 with news that a fleet of nine additional ships was on its way with fresh supplies and 500 new colonists, including women and children. But along with these new arrivals came word of a new leader, Governor Thomas West, Lord De La Warr, whom Virginia Company officials had selected to administer the colony. As governor, he would replace the system of governor and council. Despite two years of struggles and little payoff, company officials were nowhere near ready to give up on Jamestown. They were, however, ready to give up on Captain Smith. The English leader had always, by the preferences of company officials, been the wrong man to lead the colony. He had never been one to play politics and was seen as too abrupt and impatient. (It is certainly true that Captain John Smith did not like to suffer fools.) Plus, Smith was, to many company officials, a commoner, not a man born to lead. There had been no gold discovered, and despite Smith's extensive explorations during the summer of 1608, the Northwest Passage had not been discovered. The captain had dealt strongly, even harshly with the Indians. While West had not sailed with the fleet, intending to come over later, he had sent someone to lead in his place until he arrived—Sir Thomas Gates. As for Smith, it was clear that he would be playing a reduced role in Jamestown. He could not have known then that his very days in the colony he had helped found were numbered.

The first of the nine ships arrived on August 11, when four of them sailed up the James River to the fort. Since Smith's year-long tenure as president had another month to go, Smith refused to surrender his authority, as Gates himself was not on board any of these ships. The ships had crossed in mid-summer, suffered storms and heatstroke (40 had died on the voyage, including two infant boys, born at sea), and had become separated along the way.

Additional ships arrived in the days that followed. As for Gates, his ship had wrecked on an island in the Bermuda chain, although his fate was unknown to anyone in Jamestown. Those on board did not reach Jamestown until May 1610.

In Gates's absence, Francis West, the brother of Thomas, was chosen to lead the colony. West had arrived in the fall of 1608 on one of Captain Newport's ships. He was younger than Smith by six or seven years and had not proved himself during his months in Jamestown, but he had the all-important connections and name. The young West tried to institute his control over the colony as if Smith did not even exist.

As for the demoted Captain Smith, he continued to carry out important duties for the colony. He had sent groups out months earlier to establish new settlement sites, and in late summer, he went upriver to check on one of those "hivings out." There, he found a fort that colonists had built too close to the river and that was in danger of flooding. Its inhabitants had also managed to mistreat the local Indians. When Smith suggested the fort should be moved away from the offended Indians, its occupants refused, sending the captain on his way. Soon after Smith left, a small party of Indians attacked the remote settlement and killed several colonists. The survivors tracked down Smith and pleaded with him to return to their fort. Only Smith's presence managed to send the attacking Indians away.

AN UNFORTUNATE ACCIDENT

Captain Smith then sailed back down the James River toward Jamestown, which had served as his rough-hewn home for more than two years. His future in the colony was uncertain, but an accident soon determined his fate in Virginia. Arriving back in Jamestown, the captain chose to spend the night on his boat, taking a place on the deck

THE STARVING TIME

During the first two years of English colonization at Jamestown, Captain Smith had become something of the colony's "glue." He had held the colony together, and when he departed in the fall of 1609, the colonists soon experienced their roughest times yet.

Just prior to Smith's departure in October 1609, 400 new colonists had arrived at Fort James. They found the colony in disarray. There was little food, and housing was scant and inadequate. There was little true leadership or order within the settlement. The new arrivals, many weakened from their transatlantic voyage, never recovered once they arrived, and death, once more, was commonplace along the James River.

Life in Jamestown became one of desperation and starvation. Local Indians turned against the village and menaced the inhabitants regularly. They roamed the woods around the little English community, keeping the settlers trapped inside the walls of the fort. In addition, the Indians killed the Jamestown livestock, destroying another food source.

The horrors of that winter of 1609–1610, often called the Starving Time, slowly reduced the number of residents. One colonist wrote of the dreadful experience: "We were constrained to eat dogs, cats, rats, snakes, toadstools, horsehides, and what not; one man out of the misery endured, killing his wife, powdered [salted] her up to eat her, for which he was burned. Many besides fed on the corpses of dead men." One resident became so accustomed to eating human flesh that he developed an appetite for it and had to be executed by the colonists. By the spring of 1610, the population of Jamestown had been reduced from nearly 600 inhabitants to 60.

where, notes historian Benjamin Woolley, "an autumn dew collecting on the tarpaulin pulled over his shoulders." Sometime during his sleep, someone carelessly loosed a spark, perhaps from a pipe or a musket match cord, which landed on the powder bag Captain Smith was still wearing. The bag of gunpowder ignited, which "tore the flesh from his body and thighs, nine or 10 inches square in a most pitifull manner; but to quench the tormenting fire he leaped over-boord into the deepe river." Badly burned from the incident, Smith almost drowned before being pulled from the cold waters of the James. His comrades took him into Jamestown, but there was no doctor available. The surgeon, Walter Russell, who had treated Smith following his stingray poisoning a year earlier, was not present, nor was the other doctor in the colony. Ironically, they had probably relocated to one of the new settlements Smith had created the previous spring in order to help the colony survive. The captain's wounds were quite severe, and the pain caused Smith to hallucinate. One of his visions was of an assassin who pointed a pistol at him but stopped himself from firing, having taken pity on the hapless captain. (Some historians think such an assassin might have actually existed and that Smith was not hallucinating at all.)

Ultimately, his wound helped Smith to see his future. He had made what contributions he was going to make to Jamestown, and he was no longer, in the minds of company officials, needed. He was still struggling to instill complete discipline among the colonists. Relations with the Indians had seemed to deteriorate of late. There were new rumblings of an imminent attack by the Spanish. Things had never gone perfectly in Jamestown, but the problems seemed to be mounting. By early September, just days before the official end of his year tenure as president of the colony, he sent word to each of the captains of six of the ships that had delivered the hundreds of new arrivals that he wanted to sail on one of them back to England.

In 1610, Thomas West was selected governor of Virginia. West died during a voyage back to Virginia.

But when Smith's detractors in the colony learned he was leaving, they were more concerned with what stories he might tell to company officials than they were relieved to finally be rid of him. The departure of the ships was held up for weeks while accusations against Smith were collected, claims that included everything from nearly letting the colonists starve to trying to kill one of the German conspirators with rat poison. For three weeks, the accusations were collected. It all would come to nothing, of course. By October, five of the ships were ready to leave, and Smith was on board. He wrote nothing of the moment he left Jamestown behind for the last time that cool fall day in 1609. Whether he stood on the deck of the ship that was carrying him home and watched until Jamestown receded in the distance until completely out of sight is unknown. But if he was there, watching as the ships slipped between the banks of the James River toward the great bay and into open waters, he was viewing a land he had come to know well, even intimately. He had sailed to America almost three years earlier. Now he had played his part in the high drama of seventeenth-century English colonization in the New World. Captain Smith could not know it at the time, but Jamestown would survive, even if barely, due in no small part to the contributions he had made.

With his departure came one separation that may well have given him pause. The young Indian princess, Pocahontas, had become one of his constant friends. They had not seen one another regularly, but they had developed a clear companionship. It is unlikely they were ever more than friends, but, especially for Pocahontas, Smith would continue to hold a place in her heart, one made more poignant by the lie she was told after the captain's departure. Rather than tell their Indian neighbors that Smith had left the colony and returned to England, colonists told them that he had died of his injuries. It was a lie that devastated her, one she would continue to believe for years to come. As for Jamestown, it meant nothing to her without Captain Smith's presence. She turned away from having anything to do with the colony and did not return to Jamestown for four years.

8

New and Distant Shores

By the time Smith reached London, the great seventeenth-century city of 250,000 residents, he had been away for three years. Little is known of Smith's comings and goings over the next two years. He busied himself with the writing of his *Map of Virginia*, which included information about the colony and the Indians who lived nearby, including their customs and social structures, all of which would have seemed quite exotic to the typical Londoner. Published in 1612, the book included Smith's Virginia map, which remained the best version of the landscape of Virginia through the mid-1700s.

Smith took advantage of his literary forum to blast away at those early colonists who had been lazy and had not contributed significantly to the colony; men who had grumbled constantly "because they found not

English cities, nor such faire houses . . . with feather beds and downe pillows, Tavernes and alehouses in every breathing place, neither such plenty of gold and silver and dissolute liberty as they expected." Otherwise, he touted his own successes in making treaties with nearly three dozen Indian chiefs. He also spoke highly of Virginia, observing, "The mildnesse of the aire, the fertilitie of the soile, and the situation of the rivers are so propitious to the nature and use of man as no place is more convenient for pleasure, profit, and mans sustenance." Even though he was no longer working for the Virginia Company, here was Smith still recruiting would-be colonists.

He kept his ear to the ground, questioning those who returned on ships directly from the Chesapeake region, picking up little bits of information about Jamestown and its survival. He learned that the winter of 1609–1610 had been the most miserable of them all, with starving colonists forced to commit acts of cannibalism. He also learned that the colonists had come close to completely abandoning Virginia, only to encounter rescue ships at the mouth of the James just as they were intent on sailing back to England. Captain Smith also heard the news of the introduction of tobacco growing in Virginia, brought about by a colonist named John Rolfe. Rolfe had discovered that Caribbean tobacco grew well in Virginia and, if the leaves were dried properly, retained its sweet, full flavor. As tobacco was highly popular in England at the time, the weed became the colony's salvation as a cash crop. Smith, however, was not happy with this turn of events, as he considered smoking a filthy habit.

Smith remained for four years in England, longing to return to America. Company officials were not interested in reemploying him, so his possibilities were limited. Smith began to consider other lands in the New World and fell upon the region of New England. He began

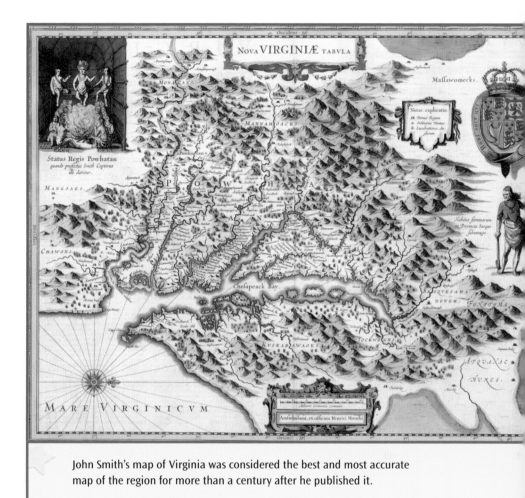

John Smith's map of Virginia was considered the best and most accurate map of the region for more than a century after he published it.

drumming up capital for a colonial venture, managing to get agreements from four London merchants to pony up monies for a couple of ships and provisions. During the early months of 1614, he excitedly made plans to return to America. By the end of February, the ships were readied, setting sail down the Thames River, with Smith commanding one and Captain Thomas Hunt in charge of the other. Now 34 years old, Smith was headed back to sea, once again bound for the New World. Among those on board was an Indian named Squanto,

SMITH DELIVERS AN INDIAN HOME

As Captain Smith set sail in 1614 for America, bound for New England, he took along with him a special passenger, an Indian named Squanto. The Native American's story is its own special adventure. A member of the Pawtuxet tribe, Squanto had been taken on an English fishing vessel to England in 1605. There he had lived until 1614, spending several years in London. Ready to return home, he caught a ride on Smith's ship.

But Squanto's adventure was not over. A short time after his return to New England, he was kidnapped, this time by the notorious Captain Thomas Hunt, and sold into slavery in Spain. In time, Squanto escaped and returned to England. By 1619, he was delivered back to New England. Upon his return, he was saddened to find his former village had been wiped out by smallpox. Without a tribe or a home, Squanto had joined the Wampanoag, a neighboring Indian nation in modern-day Massachusetts. He

who had spent several years in England. He was from New England, and Smith agreed to return him to his native lands.

NEW ENGLAND

By April 1614, the two ships reached Monhegan Island off the coast of today's Maine, close to the mouth of the Kennebec River. The Popham colony had been built nearby. Those Englishmen whom Smith had recruited, all sponsored by London merchants, were expected to deliver a profit to those who held the purse strings. Orders had been given to search for whales, as well as gold and copper. If such efforts failed, they were to collect fish and trade for furs from the Indians.

served as an adviser and interpreter for his adopted tribe's leader, a sachem (chief) named Massasoit.

Squanto's path would cross that of other Englishmen soon after his arrival back in New England. In late 1620, a shipload of English colonists arrived at a site along the Massachusetts coast. History remembers them as the Pilgrims, who anchored their ship, the *Mayflower*, off the coast of lands they would call Plymouth. Able to speak English, the Indian who had been to England more than once provided valuable help to the new English arrivals. He taught them how to live off the bounty of the New England landscape, including how to plant corn and where to fish. Thus, Squanto made historical contact with not only Captain Smith, but those who would eventually plant the first successful English colony in New England. The lives of Smith, Squanto, and the Pilgrims came together through an unlikely interconnectedness of events in America.

These Englishmen were not alone as the original Jamestown colonists had been seven years earlier. Monhegan was a familiar place, a site where as many as 200 ships might land during a single fishing season. The men set about searching for whales. Smith wrote later: "We saw many and spent much time in chasing them; but could not kill any." Some men searched for gold, but with no more success than the colonists at Jamestown had. By the time the new arrivals turned to harvesting fish and fur, the peak season had passed. The men had managed to catch 50,000 pounds (22,680 kg) of fish in two months, and more than 1,000 beaver pelts were taken, but it was not enough to represent a profit.

As for Smith, he participated in none of these activities but spent much time doing what he had come to enjoy during his time in

Virginia—explore. He ventured along the northern coast in a small boat, poking around in various bays and inlets, just as he had done along the James, Pamunkey, Potomac, and other Virginia waterways. Smith was unaccustomed to considering America as a place simply to tap the natural resources. Jamestown had been intended as a permanent colony for the English. He was now intent on discovering a suitable place for another such settlement site. Smith had become convinced that the New World represented great opportunities for England's common men, those similar in background to himself. As he wrote later, it was here, in America, that a man could carve out a place for himself, regardless of background, with "onely his merit to advance his fortunes."

With his Jamestown experiences to fall back on, he could imagine what others might not. He wrote later of the things that came to mind as he explored, of the opportunities the wilderness offered to industrious people. He even worked out a basic plan: Those English ships that came regularly to New England waters to fish could begin delivering settlers and colonists who would work as fish driers and packers. This would provide an economic base on which to build the colony. When the great ships were filled with their season's catch, they could depart for England and leave their smaller fishing vessels behind in the care of the settlers. England could be transplanted into North America at one more location. This view of creating a new place of permanent English occupation led Captain Smith to create the name by which the region is still known today—New England.

His explorations included Penobscot Bay, which he mapped as he floated its estuaries. He took a trip as far as 40 miles (64 km) up the Kennebec River, noting the "great high clifts of barren Rocks overgrowne with Wood." The Maine coastline he described as "a Countrie rather to affright, then delight one." He explored bays and shoals, islands and inlets. He sailed south to the Massachusetts coastline and was duly impressed with the landscape before him, calling it "the Paradise of all those parts," a land featuring great woods and good harbors. He had learned the difficulties of settling in a marsh, so when he arrived at today's Boston Bay, he became ecstatic, seeing it as a place providing a natural defense. Then he reached a site that appeared destined for English occupation. He observed before him "an excellent good harbor, good land; and no want of anything but industrious people." It would be named Plymouth. Six years later, Puritans from England, remembered as the Pilgrims, arrived on board their ship, *Mayflower*, and established themselves at that very location.

Just as in Virginia, Captain Smith made contact with the local Indians, including the Massachusetts nation. As they spoke an Algonquian dialect, Smith was able to converse with some of them in what he later described as "a broken language." It was all so reminiscent of his days in Virginia that he became as excited about the potential the land represented as he had been about launching an expedition to New England months earlier. By July, the fishing season over, his ship headed back toward England loaded with fish oil, salt fish, and furs, including beaver, otter, and martin. The second ship left later, carrying a cargo of dried fish, bound for Spain. Smith would later learn that Captain Hunt had tricked the Indian Squanto onto his ship and kidnapped him, only to sell him as a slave to the Spanish. Smith was angered by the news, fearing Hunt's actions might have angered the local Indians so much that they would never allow a settlement to be established. Captain Smith later described Hunt as "a worthlesse fellow of our Nation."

Soon, Smith began advertising his plan for a permanent colony in New England. After several stops and starts and failed promises, investors were secured. A ship of 200 tons (181 metric tons) was procured, a large vessel of that day, along with a smaller ship of 50 tons (45 t). Smith began signing up men for his settlement. Several agreed to join the expedition, but only 16 contracted to remain in New England with Smith to make a go of his colony. In some ways, his short list of colonists was similar to those who had sailed with him to found Fort James in 1607. They included 14 men and two boys, including gentlemen, soldiers, and laborers. Smith and his men set sail for America in March 1615, with the seasoned captain on the deck watching the port recede into the distance as he left England for yet another adventure.

DANGEROUS WATERS

Immediately, trouble stalked the ships as strong winds blew into a gale that separated the two vessels. The masts on the large ship were broken and its hull badly damaged, necessitating its return to port. A replacement ship was arranged, a smaller vessel of 60 tons (54 t). Smith and his men, including 16 colonists and a crew of 14 sailors, set sail again on June 24. The next problem Smith faced was with pirates. The Atlantic was a great ocean of piracy in the early seventeenth century, with many an English pirate preying on hapless Spanish treasure ships. Suddenly, a pirate vessel was bearing down on Smith's ship. For two days, a chase unfolded. Smith was unable to escape, and the pirates caught up with and boarded the would-be colonizing vessel.

What a surprise awaited Captain Smith when he discovered that the pirates boarding his ship included men whom he had commanded during his days as a mercenary during the Turkish wars. Immediately, the men were ready to allow Smith and his party to go on their way. They even offered to join with him in his latest venture. But Smith continued on without them.

Sailing past the Azores, Smith again was set upon, this time by four French warships. Although Smith and his men prepared to put up a fight, they soon learned the French were Protestants with orders

Pirates attack a British navy ship in this seventeenth-century painting. John Smith was involved in his share of piracy on his way to the New World.

to harass only Spanish and Portuguese vessels, as well as pirate ships. They invited Smith to join them in their flagship, only to take him prisoner. Having carried out a ruse, the French vessels pressed Smith's ship into action as part of their squadron, dividing his men between the five vessels. After six days or so, the French finally allowed Smith and his men to rejoin their ship and continue their voyage. While they returned all the provisions they had commandeered earlier, they did not give back most of the weapons they had taken.

Smith knew he would have to recollect the confiscated weapons before taking their full leave of the French. Before he was able to do so, the French fell upon several ships, set on plunder. Smith had little recourse but to stay attached to the French pirates. Finally, the prize the French had been looking for showed up in the distance, a fleet of Spanish ships from the West Indies. As Smith and his men had no appreciation for the Spanish, they agreed to participate in the attack. For all practical purposes, Captain John Smith had embarked on a new, if temporary, career—that of a pirate.

The attack went well for the French and Smith's vessel. During a four- or five-hour exchange of cannon fire, the French defeated several Spanish ships, yielding prizes that included thousands of animal skins, 370 chests of sugar, and 38,000 ryals, known popularly as pieces of eight. (These were wedge-shaped pieces of Spanish dollars, equal to approximately one-eighth of the original coin.) This gave Smith a taste of the pirate life, which he continued through the following months until October. The captain probably expected to receive a share of the spoils for him and his men, but it was not to be. By November, the French fleet landed in their home port of La Rochelle. They then turned on Smith (they had no purpose for him any longer) and not only refused to give him his share of the captured prizes, but accused him of having burned a French colonial settlement in modern-day Canada. Smith, of course, had done nothing of the sort. Uncertain of his fate, Smith decided to escape. Under cover of darkness, he commandeered a rowboat and headed out to sea.

Smith's bad luck continued, and his small craft fell into a great storm, the caravel rising and falling on giant waves. The storm continued for 12 hours, with Captain Smith desperately trying to keep his tiny boat afloat. He was finally thrown onto an island and, after pawning his little craft, made his way back to La Rochelle. There, he was surprised to find that the French pirates' flagship had gone down in the same storm he had struggled through, along with its valuable cargo. Before the end of the year, after months of frustration, storms, delay, and piracy, Captain Smith was back in England. He later discovered that some of his men had also found their way free from the French and had reached Plymouth.

9

Smith Reunites with Pocahontas

By June 1616, Smith was as busy as he had ever been in England. His book, *A Description of New England*, came into print, a small work of 64 pages. He also received word that a party from Jamestown had landed in Plymouth, England, and would soon be in London. Among the new arrivals was his young friend among the Powhatan peoples—Pocahontas.

Much had happened to Smith's young acquaintance during the captain's seven-year absence from Jamestown. For four years, she had not returned to Jamestown, having been informed that Smith was dead. By 1611, she was living in the village of the Patawomeck, approximately 65 miles (105 km) from Werowocomoco, in the care of a chief allied to her father. When a pair of English traders reached the village, they learned of

Pocahontas's presence and worked up a plot to kidnap her for the purpose of exchanging her for some English captives held by her father. After Powhatan returned the captives, but not some tools and weapons his warriors had also taken, the English kept Pocahontas, holding her for a year. Apparently she was well-treated and even converted to Christianity, taking the English name Rebecca following her baptism. By the spring of 1614, Pocahontas had an opportunity to meet with some of her people. She spoke against her father, accusing him of valuing her "less than old swords, pieces, or axes." Pocahontas told her fellow tribe members to tell Powhatan she was going to remain with the English.

It was during her "captivity" that Pocahontas met John Rolfe, a widower who had introduced Caribbean tobacco as a successful cash crop to Virginia. The two married on April 5, 1614, in the little wooden church at Jamestown, then settled on Rolfe's plantation, Varina Farms, situated along the banks of the James River. On January 30, 1615, a son, Thomas, was born. A peripheral result of the marriage between the English colonist and the Indian princess was a peaceful period that followed.

Now Pocahontas and Rolfe were in England, headed by coach toward London, along with 11 other people from Powhatan's nation. In addition to becoming a Christian, she had learned the English language and English customs and social mores.

THE REUNION

Meanwhile, Smith's new book, *A Description of New England*, was coming into print. He sent a copy to Prince Charles and then wrote a letter to Queen Anne, explaining how Pocahontas had saved his life in Virginia and helped keep the colony alive by supplying food. He asked the queen to give the Indian woman a royal welcome.

Thinking John Smith was dead, Pocahontas married John Rolfe. On a visit to England, the two were guests of the court of King James, and later Pocahontas was reunited with her old friend.

Smith traveled to Brentford, a small town just outside of London, to see his old friend. It is not clear when exactly he went, but it appears he did not go immediately after Pocahontas's arrival. He was busy at the time with new plans for a voyage to America, so perhaps that delayed his visit. He may have been embarrassed to go and see the one person from America he should have tried to make some type of contact with previously. Seven years had passed, and he had never sent a single message back to Virginia intended for Pocahontas; not a single missive to tell her of his whereabouts, his comings and goings, or even a reminiscence of their days together in Virginia.

He found her dressed not as he would have remembered her, but in the finery of a well-bred Englishwoman. The reunion began awkwardly. At first, Pocahontas seemed reserved, perhaps angry. Smith described their encounter: "After a modest salutation, without any word, she turned about, obscured her face, as not seeming well contented; and in that humour her husband, with divers others, we all left her two or three houres, repenting my selfe to have writ she could speake English. But not long after, she began to talke, and remembered mee well what courtesies shee had done."

Pocahontas reminded Smith: "You did promise Powhatan what was yours should bee his, and he the like to you; you called him father being in his land a stranger, and by the same reason so must I doe you." Smith would have none of it. He would not allow her to call him "father," reminding her she was the daughter of a king. But Pocahontas stood firm—"with a well set countenance"—and spoke again to Smith: "Were you not afraid to come into my fathers Countrie, and caused feare in him and all his people (but mee), and feare you here I should call you father? I tell you then I will, and you shall call mee childe, and so I will bee for ever and ever your Countrieman." Then she told Smith that, after his departure from Jamestown in the fall of 1609, his countrymen had told her he was dead.

These days of reunion would come to an end forever. By March 1617, John Rolfe and Pocahontas were bound for America, ready to return to Virginia. During their departure, barely down the river and out of London, Pocahontas became sick, unable to continue the trip. Soon after, she died. What exactly her ailment was is uncertain. It might have been smallpox. She may have had pneumonia or tuberculosis. But before month's end, the young Indian princess who had transformed herself into Rebecca, a married Englishwoman, died. Her husband, Rolfe, later described her death, recounting her last words as she noted that "all must die, but tis enough that her child liveth." She was buried at the parish of St. George's, Gravesend. Her death occurred just a few months short of the tenth anniversary of the arrival of three English ships along the James River, filled with eager colonists and settlers, among them, her future friend, Captain John Smith.

MORE DREAMS OF AMERICA

Captain Smith was intent on his plans for his next colonizing venture in New England. It may well have become all-consuming for him, this business of leading another expedition of Englishmen ready to settle another corner of the New World. To establish such a colony would make him more than he had been at Jamestown; he would be the actual founder of a colony, in a region he had already named. He was known in London for having established Englishmen in Virginia. No one in England had more practical, hands-on experience to bring to a colonial endeavor than Captain Smith. And he had not only learned during his years how to remake himself in the wilderness of America, he had also made himself into a grand promoter and publicist.

He had accomplished great things for Virginia. The miracle that was Jamestown owed no small debt to the contributions made by Captain Smith. Ten years after the founding of Jamestown, Smith could not help believing that his greatest achievements lay ahead of him. He was, after all, only 37 years old as 1617 opened.

With support from old and new investors and backers, Smith procured three more ships, primarily for yet another fishing and whaling expedition. But the captain signed on another 15 men to remain in New England after the fishing season was complete. It is not known whether any of them were from among those who had joined Smith in his earlier, misbegotten adventure. It appears that all things were ready by December 1616, but something delayed their departure from England. It seems that his flotilla of ships may have missed the seasonal winds. He wrote later: "I was wind-bound three months, so that the season being past, the shippes went for New-foud-land: whereby my desseigne was frustrate; which was to me and my friends, no small losse." No, indeed. If Smith was hanging everything, perhaps even his ultimate legacy, on his next expedition to New England, the failure that year must have stung and disappointed. Newfoundland was not New England, and he had no interest in fishing in Canada. Apparently he could not convince his backers to allow even one ship to make its way as far south as modern-day Maine, where Smith could have followed his dreams of his next colony. All company officials could muster in his support was bestowing a title on him, making him Admiral of New England for life.

Smith was put off by his failure to colonize in 1617 (not to mention his 1615 misadventure), but he was not discouraged to the point of giving up. However, others were not so positive. Smith lived in an age when people took signs seriously, and to such individuals, especially those gentlemen and merchants providing support for Smith's company work, the captain was gaining the reputation of having bad luck. Some began to separate themselves from him, turning to other would-be adventurers. The captain had little success getting everything lined up for another attempt at reaching New England and planting an English presence there. By the summer of 1617, the discouragement that he had avoided finally caught up with him, and he gave up recruiting backers outside London. It appears the doors were closing on the captain.

Smith's frustrations continued into the summer, as the season passed for an expedition to sail to America and carry out the dual purposes of fishing and settlement. The spring of 1618 arrived, and Smith continued to be frustrated by the lack of progress on his return to colonize in New England. He likely met that year with George

Smith was given the title Admiral of New England by his backers. This empty title did not soothe the sting he felt by his failure to set up a New England colony.

Yeardley, who had arrived in Jamestown in 1609, the same year Captain Smith had departed. While Yeardley was in London, he was knighted by King James; he set sail to return to America the following January. How much Smith may have been envious of the attention Governor Yeardley received by the Crown is unknown, but it must have rankled him. Yeardley had not been in Jamestown during its first two formative years, those during which Smith had played such a key role in helping the colony ultimately survive.

Smith would have also been aware of the significant changes taking place in Virginia at the same time. Yeardley had taken back to Jamestown his orders from Virginia Company officials to end the harsh military rule that had remained in the colony for several years. He was also supposed to establish an assembly (it would be called the House of Burgesses), which would promote representative government in Virginia. The governor was also empowered to hand out land grants to each Virginia colonist to the tune of 100 acres (40 ha) for all who had been in the colony prior to 1616 and 50 acres (20 ha) to all those who had arrived since. Perhaps Smith could take a measure of pride in such developments for Jamestown. After all, had he not provided singular leadership in its early years, the colony might not have survived to enjoy such measures of success.

SMITH AND THE PILGRIMS

Little is known specifically concerning Smith's comings and goings during these years. It is known, however, that he was approached by others who were preparing to make their way to America. In 1619, he was contacted by agents representing a sect of religious nonconformists who had read about America in Smith's own words. England's state-supported religious body was the Church of England. During the early 1600s, several other Christian sects tried to worship in their

THE PILGRIMS REACH SMITH'S NEW ENGLAND

Not only did Captain John Smith have a direct impact on the early years of Virginia and the Jamestown colony, he also left his thumbprint on New England and the Plymouth Colony. The leaders of those religious dissenters remembered today as the Pilgrims had read of New England through Smith's writings, and their agents had talked with Smith directly. The Pilgrims chose not to hire on Smith as their military leader, however, and prepared in 1620 to make the trip to America without his direct assistance.

The party of 102 would-be colonists left England in August 1620 on board two ships, the *Speedwell* and the *Mayflower*. When the *Speedwell* proved less than seaworthy, the Pilgrims had no choice but to crowd their party onto the *Mayflower* for the voyage to America. The journey proved to be one of hardship and danger. They encountered violent storms that blew them off course, with one hurricane splitting the main beam below decks and crippling the vessel, which spelled disaster. When the ship appeared doomed, the Pilgrims saved themselves by using one of their jacks, which they had loaded for the voyage to use in raising their houses in America. The beam was put back in place, and the party of colonists was saved.

When they reached the shores of New England, they searched for the sites Captain Smith had mentioned as likely locations for a settlement. They dropped anchor off Cape Cod on November 21. Over the following weeks, the Pilgrims explored the coast around Cape Cod Bay. At a site they later called Plimouth, the colonists found an abandoned Indian village, which had been struck by a smallpox epidemic a few years earlier. Smith had explored this very spot and had written of it in glowing terms. Here, the Pilgrims anchored the *Mayflower* and soon began the hard work of building their colonial outpost in the New World.

own ways in England but were persecuted by King James's agents for failing to support the Church of England. One such group was a sect whose members called themselves Puritans or Separatists. They rejected the Anglican Church's ecclesiastical practices, most of which were old Catholic practices once removed. One group of Puritans living in Scrooby, England, had previously packed up and moved to Holland so they could practice their faith according to their own beliefs. Dissatisfied with life in the Low Countries, several of them moved back to England, having decided to leave for America. They first negotiated with the Dutch for support, but those efforts fell apart. Then, they approached the London Virginia Company, again only to be rebuffed.

While searching for a viable New World opportunity, the leaders of the Puritans were introduced to the possibilities of moving to New England. And their source was one of only a few available— Captain Smith's book, *A Description of New England*. It is known for certain that the Puritan minister William Brewster had a copy of Smith's book in his library when he died in 1643. Smith's descriptions appealed to the Puritans, and Brewster would himself write that he and his followers were drawn "cheefly for the hope of present profits to be made by the fishing." It is extremely unlikely that the Scrooby Separatists would have considered the advantages of New England without Captain Smith's descriptions. Thus, John Smith had not only a direct impact on the early history of Jamestown, the first successful English colony in North America, but an important indirect influence on the establishment of the second successful English venture. At one point, Smith even made it clear to the agents representing the Puritans that he would be willing and available to go to America with them as their guide and military leader. Ultimately, though, Smith claims that the Puritan sect chose not to hire him because of the expense. The Scrooby Puritans were a relatively poor group that decided they could utilize the information found in

Smith's book without actually having to employ him. As Smith later wrote, the Puritans were so unaware and ignorant of what lay ahead for them in America that it "caused them, for more than a yeare, to endure a wonderfull deale of misery, with an infinite patience; saying my books and maps were much better cheape to teach them, than my selfe."

The captain is certainly accurate when he refers to the "misery" the Puritans experienced when they landed in New England following their voyage on the *Mayflower* in 1620. Despite what Smith might have cost them if they had hired him on, their efforts might have been eased by his presence, his leadership, and his skills and knowledge of how to colonize successfully in the New World.

The record of Smith's activities otherwise during 1620 are few, but it is known that come December, his next book, *New England Trials*, came into print. It was a pamphlet, really, at only 16 pages in length. At its center, the book was Smith's presentation on how England could go about establishing a royal navy. He used the text, though, to propose once again a new joint stock company. He carried copies with him when he went around England giving inspirational speeches in support of his proposed adventure. Again, nothing came of it. True frustration began to stalk Smith. Speech after speech, written work after written work—few seemed to have responded to his efforts. In his later writings, he expressed his increasing bitterness over it all: "These fourteene yeres I have spared neither pains nor money according to my abilitie, in the discovery of Norumbega [legendary settlement in northeastern North America]." He described how he had invested in Virginia "neare five yeares worke, and more then five hundred pound of my owne estate; beside all the dangers, miseries and encumbrances and losse of other employments I endured gratis." With each passing year, Smith was coming no closer to getting support to return to New England and start up another colony. In 1621, he turned 41.

10

The Twilight Years

In 1620, after restructuring and revitalizing, the Plymouth Company became the Council for New England, represented by 40 upper-class investors. Although Smith's old friend Ferdinando Gorges was chosen as the group's president, no call to Smith was forthcoming. Looking to establish a colony, the organization called for it to be named New-England. While Smith was not included in any of these plans, his name for the region was. The captain was not involved in these new efforts by the revitalized Plymouth Colony, probably because his dream of a new colony did not fit the company's plans. Smith, who had fought to overcome the lazy, gold-bedazzled gentlemen in early Jamestown, always envisioned a colony without such individuals.

The colony he dreamed of would be one for common men such as himself. In New England, these men would achieve success through hard work and other enterprising efforts. Such men would have the opportunity to become land-owners in the New World and would be beholden to almost no one of a higher class, including landlords to collect rents from them. They would be fishermen, working their own nets in their own boats, seeing personal profit from their labors. In time, he planned, his colonists would be able to develop a domestic ship-building industry, tapping the seemingly endless acres of woods throughout the region. The Plymouth group, on the other hand, was made up almost entirely of members of the aristocracy or well-to-do merchants who imagined a New England colony they would rule as lords, almost a direct extension of the late medieval English world.

Although Smith would not get his opportunity to bring his colo-nizing dream to fruition, the Englishmen who did come to occupy New England created an economy based on exactly the expectations of Captain Smith, complete with a reliance on fishing and, later, ship-building. Smith's vision would come true, only not with his direct involvement.

Despite his discouragement, Smith continued to hope for a future in New England or at least in Virginia. He began petition-ing London Company officials to allow his return to the Jamestown region. In addition, he appealed to officials to pay him for the ser-vices he had rendered so many years earlier. And the company did respond positively, deciding in May 1621 to "reward him either out of the Treasury here or out of the profits the generallity in Virginia." However, no payments were ever paid to Smith. He was never even reimbursed for his earlier expenses while living in Jamestown, nor did he receive any land. In reality, the London Company was soon to fall on hard times. The company no longer held the exclusive right to hold lotteries by which they could raise investment capital. As histo-rian Bradford Smith notes, "the Company was too disorganized, too poor and too discouraged to give the colonists any effective relief," not to mention someone like Captain Smith who was no longer part of the colony and whose earlier efforts some in the company had never fully appreciated.

Then, in 1622, shocking news arrived from Virginia: A massive Indian uprising, led by Smith's old nemesis, Opechancanough, Powhatan's brother, had torn through the Virginia countryside, raiding settlements up and down the James River and murdering 350 colonists. Had a friendly Indian not warned the colonists before the uprising took place, everyone in Virginia might have been killed. It was a hard blow against the London Company, and Smith's fortunes with the company were destroyed.

Smith, the eternal soldier, saw in the massacre a potential opportunity for himself, though. He suggested to company officials that he be hired to lead a party of 130 soldiers, with which he would train colonists in the military arts to defend themselves. In addition, Smith also promised to explore and discover new lands for the company. While the offer was a good one, and one that probably would have proved beneficial to the company, the captain was yet again turned down. It appears that company officials decided they simply could not afford someone of Smith's experience and expertise. What he might have accomplished if given another opportunity to further his legacy in America will never be known, for Smith was not destined ever to return to the New World, employed by the London or Plymouth companies or anyone else.

Yet even though Smith was never to step foot on the shores of Virginia or New England again, he was never far from either in his thoughts and actions. In the fall of 1622, he published a revised version of *New England Trials* that included new information on the progress of the Puritan plantation at Plymouth. Smith still held a fondness for this new foothold in America and for Jamestown, which was entering its second generation of settlement, believing each to

Opechancanough led an uprising in 1622 that resulted in the massacre of 350 Virginia colonists. Smith thought he could return to the colony and help out, but the London Company rejected his offer.

represent an important part of his life's work. He wrote of these colonies: "I may call them my children, for they have bin my wife, my hawks, my hounds, my cards, my dice, and in totall my best content, as indifferent to my heart as my left hand to my right." Perhaps he had never stated it all clearer: America was his obsession, his worst vice, and his offspring.

SMITH'S GREAT BOOK OF 1624

Captain Smith produced no longer or greater work during his career as a writer than his *Generall Historie*. It is a work of extraordinary research, the result of collecting the works of others, including published books and letters and company reports. Although he often writes of his own exploits in the work, he also pens in information that he received secondhand. Although it might be seen as a hodgepodge of many different subjects, Smith's work is of true importance concerning the history of early America.

From the start, his goal had been to tell the complete story, beginning back in the 1490s with the English-sponsored voyages to America of John Cabot and later his son, Sebastian. He included Sir Walter Raleigh's attempts to colonize and stories of Jamestown and Plymouth.

Structurally, Smith's *Generall Historie* is actually six books massed together. He covers the early voyages of exploration in Book I, then uses Book II to reprint his *Map of Virginia*. In this part of his larger work, Smith includes descriptions of the Native Americans, which makes for a decent anthropological study.

WRITER AND HISTORIAN

Over the next two years, Captain Smith spent much of his time looking backward. He was approached by company officials, those with whom he was friendly, to write a larger work on English colonization in the New World.

He put in countless hours and days working on a new edition of his earlier writings on America. When published, the work was issued as *The Generall Historie of Virginia, New-England, and the*

Book III is a reprint with some additions and subtractions of the second part of his *Map of Virginia*. In Book IV, he recounts the history of Virginia, beginning with his personal departure in 1609 until 1624, the year King James revoked the Virginia Company's charter. The fifth book tells about the history of colonizing in Bermuda, and the last book relates the history of New England through the first years of the Puritan colony at Plymouth.

Although Smith does give a considerable amount of space in his work to his own adventures and contributions to New World colonization, he also takes the opportunity to mention others and the value of their contributions. Smith, despite his intentions, did not include in his great work a complete picture of the history of the London Company, choosing instead to focus on the "hands-on" aspects of colonizing, rather than the closed-door meetings that took place in London. It is obvious in the reading of the *Generall Historie* that the part of his book that Smith enjoyed the most was the telling of his adventures, including his explorations of rivers in Virginia and New England, his exploits with Indians and battles with pirates, as well as such "mundane" excitements as planting crops in the New World. At his heart, John Smith the writer loved to tell the stories of John Smith the adventurer.

Summer Isles. It would become his magnum opus. He wrote original text, included old versions of earlier writings (in all, he quoted directly from at least 45 other documents, many of them previously published), and introduced the story of his first rescue by Pocahontas and myriad other details. He even included a special illustrated page showing some of his more extraordinary exploits during his days in Virginia, such as his capture by Powhatan's men, the resulting powwow before Powhatan over his fate, his last-second rescue by the Indian chief's daughter, and his fight with the Paspahegh chief in 1609. It was all there—the engraved scenes of Smith's adventures, the words, the history, his life's biography and personal legacy, and the ultimate success of Jamestown, the pride of England's efforts in the New World. It must have been time-consuming, yet rewarding, for the former leader of the Virginia colony, an experience that was likely two-edged. It served as a reminiscence of all he had done in those earlier years, while reminding him of how much he continued to miss America.

When the work was published, it marked something of the end of the Virginia Company as a colonizing institution. While the company continued for another six years as a trading business, its days of recruiting men, women, and children were over. Thousands had found their way to Virginia through the company, and thousands had died trying to survive in the New World, from disease, starvation, Indian attack, and a dozen other causes. In 1624, Virginia was home to only 1,200 English colonists. And of that number, only 3 had arrived at the future site of Jamestown in the spring of 1607. Perhaps that was the company's point in having Smith publish a great history of the company's efforts in America—to help revive the company itself. But it all came too late.

To an extent, the publication of Smith's great book fell under the shadow of larger events, including the death of King James I in the early spring of 1625. James had ruled throughout most of Smith's life, and those who had founded Jamestown a generation earlier had honored him by naming their settlement after him. In addition, a great plague struck London with such a ferocity that, by the summer of 1625, residents were dying at the rate of 3,000 a week. By September, large portions of the city had been abandoned as thousands of frightened residents fled in all directions into the countryside. It is not clear whether Captain Smith was living in London at the time. If so, he may have taken refuge with friends, or he may

Smith's great work, *The Generall Historie of Virginia* (1624), was not a best-seller. But it is an important primary source of the early settlements of the New World.

have made his way back to his old lands in Lincolnshire. The plague had run its course by October. Four months later, a new monarch was crowned—Charles I. Soon, England was at war with Spain. Such change and upheaval likely took away some of the attention Smith's *Generall Historie* might have won otherwise.

Despite lackluster sales, Smith continued to write during his final years. He issued a handbook of sorts designed to train English seamen. By 1627, the old soldier participated in the war with Spain as part of an expedition to the Isle of Re off the French coast, near the site of La Rochelle, where Smith had been cast onto the coast after fleeing French pirates. Little came of the campaign. Otherwise, little is known of Smith's whereabouts or what he was up to between 1627 and 1629, other than that he wrote another work, *True Travels*, which was published in 1630. The book further rounded out Smith's biography, as it served as a description of his early years, those spent as a mercenary across the European continent, years that helped prepare him for his work in the New World. (It was in this late work that Smith tells the story of the three Turks who challenged him to duels, with each losing his head.)

That same year—1630—Captain Smith turned 50. He was living out his middle age quietly, in a suburb of London known as Newgate. Although little is known of the specifics of his final months, he would be written about years later in a book by Thomas Fuller titled *Worthies of England*: "He led his old age in London, where his having a prince's mind imprisoned in a poor man's purse rendered him to the contempt of such who were not ingenuous. Yet he forted his spirits with the remembrance and relation of what formerly he had been and what he had done." So much had been taken away from him over the years. Stripped of much of the glory he should have received for his adventures and solid leadership in America, not to mention his explorations and maps, Smith could still rely on his memories of it all, and that was something no one could take from him. That he was poor goes without saying. He was barely employed—and often unemployed—during his years following his exploits in Virginia and New England. Historian Samuel Eliot Morison would be prompted to write of Smith's contributions to early America: "Few of her founders gave so much, and got so little, as Captain John Smith."

The old soldier, explorer, and New World promoter worked right up to the end of his life, busying himself with projects, taking time out to spend with good friends, and dreaming of tomorrow. When he fell ill in the summer of 1631, he kept his wits and was able to make out a will. Just before his death, Smith's final work, a reflective pamphlet on colonization titled *Advertisements for the Unexperienced Planters of New England, or Anywhere*, was published. Death came quietly, with Captain Smith passing on June 21, 1631.

The pages of American history are littered with the names of those who, through dedication, skill, perseverance, chance, opportunity, or sheer luck, managed to leave their mark. John Smith left his through each of those circumstances. Other names would loom larger than his over the four centuries that have passed since that fateful May of 1607, when three small ships reached the waters of the New World. But few men contributed more to those first fledgling steps of the English, whose efforts would eventually bring about the founding of 13 colonies in North America, than Captain Smith. Throughout his life, he had put his humble origins behind him and had mounted the stage of history to become the one man who may be most credited with founding an English presence along the Atlantic coast. For John Smith, life was an adventure.

Chronology

1500s	The Spanish Empire dominates colonization in the Americas.
1558	Queen Elizabeth I comes to the throne of England.
1577	Elizabeth I sends "sea dog" Francis Drake to engage in raids against Spanish treasure ships in the Caribbean.

TIMELINE

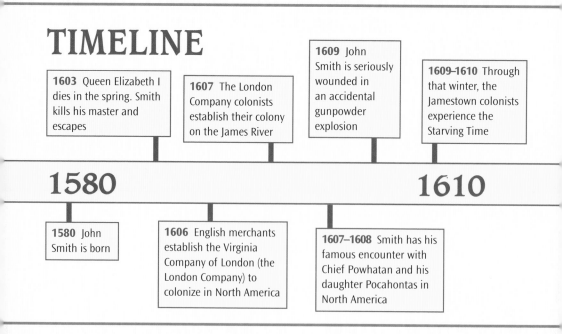

1603 Queen Elizabeth I dies in the spring. Smith kills his master and escapes

1607 The London Company colonists establish their colony on the James River

1609 John Smith is seriously wounded in an accidental gunpowder explosion

1609–1610 Through that winter, the Jamestown colonists experience the Starving Time

1580

1610

1580 John Smith is born

1606 English merchants establish the Virginia Company of London (the London Company) to colonize in North America

1607–1608 Smith has his famous encounter with Chief Powhatan and his daughter Pocahontas in North America

1580s	English sea captains and adventurers begin challenging Spanish power in the New World by expanding English trade.
1580	John Smith is born.
1583	Englishman Sir Humphrey Gilbert reaches Newfoundland to establish a New World trade colony. His efforts fail.
1584	Following Gilbert's death at sea, Elizabeth I grants right to colonize in the New World to his half brother, Sir Walter Raleigh. That summer, Raleigh sends a group to search for a New World colonial site.
1585	Raleigh sends colonists to settle on Roanoke Island off the coast of modern-day North Carolina.

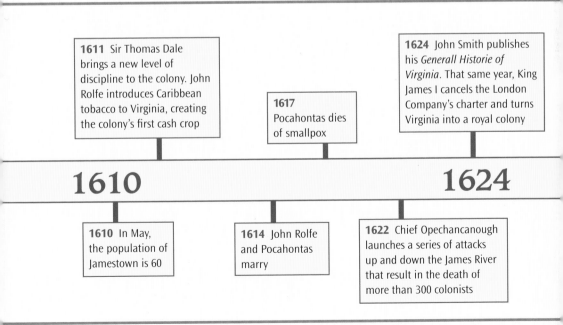

1611 Sir Thomas Dale brings a new level of discipline to the colony. John Rolfe introduces Caribbean tobacco to Virginia, creating the colony's first cash crop

1617 Pocahontas dies of smallpox

1624 John Smith publishes his *Generall Historie of Virginia*. That same year, King James I cancels the London Company's charter and turns Virginia into a royal colony

1610   1624

1610 In May, the population of Jamestown is 60

1614 John Rolfe and Pocahontas marry

1622 Chief Opechancanough launches a series of attacks up and down the James River that result in the death of more than 300 colonists

1586	Raleigh's Roanoke Colony fails. He begins plans for a second colony.
1587	Raleigh sends second group of colonists to Roanoke.
1590	The second colony at Roanoke vanishes. No permanent English colony in North America has yet been founded.
1597	Smith's father dies. Smith decides to become a soldier and fights for Dutch independence from Spain.
1600	Smith joins Austrian forces to fight the Turks in the Long War.
1602	English adventurers and merchants establish Popham colony in modern-day New England. While fighting in Transylvania, Smith is taken captive and sold as a slave.
1603	Queen Elizabeth I dies in the spring. Smith kills his master and escapes.
1604	King James I of England establishes a treaty with Spain that recognizes the right of English merchants to deliver their ships to Spanish colonies for trade. That same year, Smith returns from his years as a mercenary soldier in eastern Europe.
1606	English merchants establish the Virginia Company of Plymouth and the Virginia Company of London (the London Company) to colonize in North America. By year's end,

the London Company is ready to deliver colonists to America. Their three ships set sail in December for the New World.

1607   May   The London Company colonists establish their colony on the James River.

June   Captain Newport and Captain Smith lead a party of men to explore the James River.

September   Half of the 104 English colonists at Jamestown have died.

1607–1608   Winter   Smith has his famous encounter with Chief Powhatan and his daughter Pocahontas.

1608   Popham colony in New England fails.

January   Only 38 of the original 144 men who sailed to establish a colony at Jamestown the previous year are still alive. Later that year, Smith pens his first important report of Jamestown, *A True Relation of Such Occurrences and Accidents of Noate as Hath Hapned in Virginia.*

Summer   Smith explores the region of Chesapeake Bay.

September   Smith is elected president of the Jamestown Council.

October   Smith strengthens the colony by improving discipline and practices at Jamestown.

1609   January   Relations between Smith and Powhatan break down.

London Company officials convince King James I to abolish the local council government of Jamestown in favor of one-man rule—a governor. That fall, John Smith is seriously wounded in an accidental gunpowder explosion. By October, Smith is taken back to England to recover, never to see Jamestown again.

1609–1610   Through that winter, the Jamestown colonists experience the Starving Time.

1610   In May, the population of Jamestown is 60, approximately 10 percent of the 600 people who had arrived in Jamestown as colonists over the previous three years. Sir Thomas Dale and Sir Thomas Gates are sent to Jamestown to get the colony on its feet.

June   Even as the remnant colonists are preparing to abandon Jamestown, new colonists arrive under the leadership of Governor Lord De La Warr.

1611   March   De La Warr leaves Jamestown, replaced by Sir Thomas Dale, who brings a new level of discipline to the colony. This same year, English colonial leader John Rolfe introduces Caribbean tobacco to Virginia, creating the colony's first cash crop.

1612   Smith publishes *A Map of Virginia*.

1613   In an English raid, Chief Powhatan's daughter Pocahontas is taken as a prisoner to Jamestown.

1614	John Rolfe and Pocahontas marry. Smith returns to America, this time to explore New England.
1615	Smith's attempt to establish a colony in New England fails.
1616	Smith publishes *A Description of New England*.
1616–1617	John Rolfe takes Pocahontas to England. She and Smith are reunited. During her tour, Pocahontas dies of smallpox.
1617	Smith's second attempt to colonize in New England fails.
1618	Jamestown and Virginia colonists produce almost 50,000 pounds (22,680 kg) of tobacco for export. That same year, Chief Powhatan dies.
1619	Smith offers to lead the Pilgrims to the New World but is turned down.
1620	English colonists aboard the *Mayflower* land at Plymouth, New England. Smith publishes *New England Trials*.
1622	March Chief Opechancanough launches a series of attacks up and down the James River that result in the death of more than 300 colonists.
1624	John Smith publishes his *Generall Historie of Virginia*. That same year, King James I cancels the London Company's charter and turns Virginia into a royal colony.

1626   Smith publishes *An Accidence, or the Pathway to Experience Necessary for all Young Seamen.*

1630   Smith publishes *The True Travels, Adventures, and Observations of Captaine John Smith in Europe, Asia, Africa and America.*

1631   Smith publishes *Advertisements for the Unexperienced Planters of New England, or Anywhere.* He dies on June 21.

Bibliography

Applebaum, Robert, and John Wood Street. *Envisioning an English Empire: Jamestown and the Making of the North Atlantic World.* Philadelphia: University of Pennsylvania Press, 2005.

Athearn, Robert G. *The New World.* New York: Choice Publishing, 1988.

Bridenbaugh, Carl. *Jamestown, 1544–1699.* New York: Oxford University Press, 1980.

Dufour, Ronald P. *Colonial America.* Minneapolis, Minn.: West Publishing Company, 1994.

Gill, Harold B., and Ann Finlayson. *Colonial Virginia.* Nashville: Thomas Nelson, Inc., 1973.

Hamor, Ralph. *A True Discourse of the Present Estate of Virginia.* 1615. Reprinted in *Jamestown Narratives,* edited by Edward Wright Haile. Champlain, Va.: Roundhouse Press, 1998.

Hoffer, Peter Charles. *The Brave New World: A History of Early America.* Boston: Houghton Mifflin Company, 2000.

Horn, James. *A Land as God Made It: Jamestown and the Birth of America.* New York: Basic Books, 2005.

Horwitz, Tony. *A Voyage Long and Strange: Rediscovering the New World.* New York: Henry Holt and Company, 2008.

McNeese, Tim. *The American Colonies.* St. Louis, Mo.: Milliken Publishing Company, 2002.

Milton, Giles. *Big Chief Elizabeth: The Adventures and Fate of the First English Colonists in America.* New York: Farrar, Straus and Giroux, 2000.

Morison, Samuel Eliot. *The European Discovery of America: The Southern Voyages, A.D. 1492–1616*. New York: Oxford University Press, 1974.

Philbrick, Nathaniel. *Mayflower: A Story of Courage, Community, and War*. New York: Viking Penguin, 2006.

Smith, Bradford. *Captain John Smith: His Life & Legend*. Philadelphia: J.B. Lippincott, 1953.

Smith, John. *The Generall Historie of Virginia, New-England, and the Summer Isles*. Ann Arbor, Mich.: University Microfilms, Inc., 1966.

Snell, Tee Loftin. *The Wild Shores: America's Beginnings*. Washington, D.C.: National Geographic Society, 1974.

Southern, Ed, ed. *The Jamestown Adventure: Accounts of the Virginia Colony, 1605–1614*. Winston-Salem, N.C.: John F. Blair, Publisher, 2004.

Syme, Ronald. *John Smith of Virginia*. New York: William Morrow and Company, 1954.

Thompson, John M., ed. *The Journals of Captain John Smith: A Jamestown Biography*. Washington, D.C.: National Geographic Adventure Classics, 2007.

Further Resources

Carbone, Elisa. *Blood on the River: James Town, 1607.* New York: Penguin Group, 2007.

Doherty, Kieran. *To Conquer Is to Live: The Life of Captain John Smith of Jamestown.* Minneapolis, Minn.: Lerner Publishing Group, 2001.

Fritz, Jean. *Double Life of Pocahontas.* New York: Penguin Group, 2002.

Hoobler, Dorothy. *Captain John Smith: Jamestown and the Birth of the American Dream.* Indianapolis, Ind.: John Wiley and Sons, 2005.

Loker, Aleck. *Fearless Captain: The Adventures of John Smith.* Greensboro, N.C.: Morgan Reynolds Publishers, 2006.

McNeese, Tim. *Jamestown.* New York: Chelsea House Publishers, 2007.

Mello, Tara Baukus. *John Smith.* Broomall, Pa.: Chelsea House Publishers, 2000.

Petrie, Kristin. *John Smith.* Edina, Minn.: ABDO Publishing Company, 2007.

WEB SITES

Chesapeake Bay Program: Captain John Smith
http://www.chesapeakebay.net/jsmith.htm

Colonial Williamsburg: Captain John Smith
http://www.history.org/foundation/journal/smith.cfm

Eyewitness to History: Captain John Smith Is Saved by Pocahontas, 1608
http://www.eyewitnesstohistory.com/johnsmith.htm

Gloucester County History: Werowocomoco Indians
http://www.co.gloucester.va.us/indians1.htm

History Globe: The Jamestown Online Adventure
http://www.historyglobe.com/jamestown

Jamestown Rediscovery
http://www.apva.org/jr.html

Jamestown Rediscovery: Captain John Smith
*http://www.preservationvirginia.org/history/jsmith.html?
process=0*

Jamestown Settlement
http://www.historyisfun.org/jamestown/jamestown.cfm

Powhatan Renape Nation: The Pocahontas Myth
http://www.powhatan.org/pocc.html

The Real Pocahontas
http://pocahontas.morenus.org

The Story of Virginia: Contact and Conflict
http://www.vahistorical.org/sva2003/pocahontas.htm

United States History John Smith
http://www.u-s-history.com/pages/h713.html

Werowocomoco Research Project
http://powhatan.wm.edu

Picture Credits

79: John Smith's *Map of Virginia*, published in Amsterdam, c. 1630 (engraving), Hondius, Henrik I (1573–p. 1649)/ Virginia Historical Society, Richmond, Virginia, USA/ The Bridgeman Art Library Interanational

85: The Print Collector

89: Library of Congress, Prints and Photographs Division, LC-USZC2-6370

93: *Captain John Smith* (1580–1631) (coloured engraving), Passe, Simon de (1595–1647) / Private Collection/Peter Newark American Pictures/ The Bridgeman Art Library International

101: The massacre of the settlers in 1622, plate VII, from *America, Part XIII*, German edition, 1628 (coloured engraving), Merian, Matthaus, the Elder (1593–1650)/ Virginia Historical Society, Richmond, Virginia, USA/ The Bridgeman Art Library International

105: Title page from John Smith, *The Generall Historie of Virginia, New England and the Summer Isles*, 1624 (engraving), American School, (17th century)/Virginia Historical Society, Richmond, Virginia, USA/The Bridgeman Art Library International

Index

About the Author

Tim McNeese is an associate professor of history and a department chair at York College in York, Nebraska. McNeese is a graduate of York College, Harding University, and Missouri State University. He has published more than 110 books and educational materials. His writing has earned him a citation in the library reference work *Contemporary Authors* and multiple citations in *Best Books for Young Teen Readers*. In 2006, Tim appeared on the History Channel program *Risk Takers, History Makers: John Wesley Powell and the Grand Canyon*. He has been a faculty member at the Tony Hillerman Writers Conference in Albuquerque. His wife, Beverly, is an assistant professor of English at York College. They have two married children, Noah and Summer, and four grandchildren—Ethan, Adrianna, Finn William, and Beckett. The McNeeses have sponsored college study trips along the Lewis and Clark Trail, through the American Southwest, and to New England. You may contact Professor Tim McNeese at tdmcneese@york.edu.